Home Plate COOKBOOK

Recipes from baseball greats— just great for your home plate

by Gary Saunders

CRANE HILL
PUBLISHERS

Birmingham, Alabama

Published by Crane Hill Publishers, 3608 Clairmont Avenue, Birmingham, AL 35222; www.cranehill.com

Printed in the United States of America

Library of Congress Cataloging-in-Publication Data

Saunders, Gary.
Home plate: recipes from baseball greats just great for your home plate/by Gary Saunders.
p.   cm.
ISBN 1-57587-072-X (alk. paper)
1. Cookery, American. 2. Baseball players–United States. I. Title.
TX715.S255   1998
641.5–dc21   98-9647
                                           CIP

To my sons, Austin and Travis

May they learn to enjoy
the crack of the bat
and the sizzle of the grill
as much as their old man.

Table of Contents

Introduction

Food and baseball have been together from the very beginning. Around 1859 primitive "ball" clubs in the South set up tents to shelter their female fans from the blistering sun. A wide variety of refreshments were offered these Southern belles as they cheered on their local diamond heroes. All this before the game was even known as baseball!

During professional baseball's formative years fans could munch on what is now traditional ballpark fare—peanuts, popcorn, and soft drinks, as well as more offbeat items such as hard-boiled eggs, blocks of cheese, broiled onions, and tripe (the stomach lining of cattle). Stadium concession stands as we now know them could be found as far back as 1875. Many ballparks of this period served up cold beer as well as hard liquor. This concerned many team owners who feared that rowdy, drunken fans were keeping women and children away from the turnstiles. Open betting on games also posed problems.

In 1880 the National League passed a ruling that strictly forbade gambling and alcoholic beverages at all its parks. The Cincinnati Red Stockings, not wanting to give up their enormous alcohol revenues, departed the League and started the American Association. Fans brave enough to attend games in this so-called "Beer and Whiskey League" often had to be on the lookout for flying beer mugs and shot glasses!

Beer is now offered at all big league parks and often accounts for fifty percent of a team's concession take. In fact, beer ranks second only to hot dogs in total ballpark concession sales. For years the Anheuser–Busch Company operated the St. Louis Cardinals, and the Coors family still owns a substantial piece of Denver's Colorado Rockies. Milwaukee's reputation as the "Beer Capital of the U.S." led to its franchise being dubbed the Brewers in 1970. Miller

Park, named for the Miller Brewing Company, is scheduled to open in Milwaukee in the year 2000.

Just like the grand old game of baseball itself, ballpark cuisine has come a long, long way. Fans now have more food and drink choices than ever before, with concession stands at stadiums across the country offering gourmet pizza, fresh seafood, cafe latte, vegetarian fare, and even sushi. Plush stadium dining rooms and luxury skyboxes, which are run by multimillion-dollar food service companies, serve shrimp cocktail, prime rib, bison burgers, pasta, and pate.

This book celebrates America's two great pastimes: baseball and eating. More than a delicious collection of recipes, Home Plate offers history, humor, and trivia as well as a special peek into the kitchens of some of baseball's biggest names past and present. Baseball people love to eat and drink, and that is reflected in the following pages.

Now don your chef's hat, fire up the grill, grab hold of some cooking utensils, and step up to the plate. With the recipes and anecdotes in *Home Plate,* you'll be a sure hit at any dinner table!

Gary Saunders
June 1998

About the Author

Gary Saunders was born and raised in northern Virginia. He graduated from Virginia Tech and has spent seven years in the professional sports industry, serving as general manager of the Meridian Brakemen, a minor league baseball team, and currently as director of ticketing for the Atlanta Braves' new Carolina League team in Myrtle Beach, South Carolina. *Home Plate* is Gary's first book.

Gary lives in the Myrtle Beach area with his wife, Eileen, their two young sons, Austin and Travis, and their Labrador retriever, Sundance.

Acknowledgments

In baseball it is said that the manager is only as good as the players. This is certainly true of me and my contributors. A heartfelt tip of the ball cap to all the fine folks who have made this project possible.

Many thanks to my cooking idols, Emeril Lagasse and Keith Floyd, for making cooking exciting, hip, and—most of all—fun.

A special thanks to my wife, Eileen, for her patience and valued assistance. To Crane Hill's Norma McKittrick for her guidance. And to my family for their unwavering support.

Home Plate
COOKBOOK

Recipes from baseball greats—
just great for your home plate

Ted Abernathy

Photograph courtesy of Ted Abernathy

L anky relief pitcher Ted Abernathy had a most unusual delivery, and this North Carolina native baffled opposing hitters with his sidewinding, submarine motion. Ted pitched for seven Major League clubs over 17 seasons. Three times he led the National League in games pitched and twice was named the League's "Fireman of the Year."

In 1965 Ted recorded 31 saves for the Cubs, but after an off year he was traded to the Cincinnati Reds in 1967. Ted rewarded Reds fans with a league-leading 28 saves and an unheard of 1.27 earned run average. He retired in 1972 with a career total of 148 saves.

Ted and his wife, Marge, reside in Gastonia, North Carolina.

Candied Sweet Potatoes

3-4 sweet potatoes, boiled, peeled, and sliced
1/2 cup white sugar
1/4 cup brown sugar
1 teaspoon cinnamon
2 eggs, beaten
1/4 cup milk
1 cup cornflakes
Brown sugar
1/2 cup butter, melted
Shredded coconut
Chopped pecans or walnuts

Preheat oven to 575°.

Combine sweet potato slices, sugars, cinnamon, eggs, and milk. Mix well and place in a greased baking dish. Top with cornflakes and sprinkle with additional brown sugar.

Pour melted butter over top, and sprinkle with coconut and chopped nuts.

Bake uncovered for 15 minutes.

Ted's Baked Chicken Breasts

2 small packages dried beef
6 chicken breasts, skinned and boned
1 can cream of mushroom soup
1 cup sour cream

Preheat oven to 200°.

Line the bottom of a baking pan with dried beef. Place chicken breasts on top of beef, and pour soup over chicken.

Cover and bake 3 1/2 hours. Remove cover and continue baking until top is brown.

Top with sour cream and serve.

Ace Adams

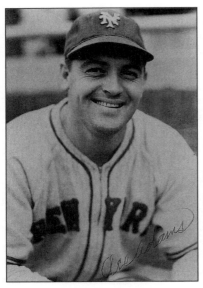

Photograph courtesy of Ace Adams

A ce Adams was born in Willows, California, in 1912. Appropriately named by his parents, Ace was one of baseball's premier relief specialists from 1941 through 1946. He spent his entire career with the New York Giants, and his teammates included Carl Hubbell, Mel Ott, and Johnny Mize.

Ace led the National League in saves for two consecutive seasons (1944 and 1945), and he established a Major League record with 70 games pitched in 1943. His life took a dramatic turn in 1946 when he jumped to the outlaw Mexican League and was subsequently banished from the Major Leagues, ending a brief yet promising career.

Ace now lives in Albany, Georgia.

Ace's Hush Puppies

1/2 cup flour
1/2 cup cornmeal
1/4 teaspoon salt
2 teaspoons baking powder
1 egg, beaten
1/4 cup water
1/4 cup minced onion
2 tablespoons red bell pepper, chopped
2 tablespoons green bell pepper, chopped
Vegetable oil, shortening, or fish grease

Mix together flour, cornmeal, salt, and baking powder. Combine egg and water; add to flour mixture. Fold in minced onion and chopped peppers; mixture will be "stiff."

Heat oil (Ace prefers fish grease) in skillet. Drop spoonfuls of mixture into hot oil, and cook until light brown.

Southwest Salsa

1 ear of corn, husked
1 (15-ounce) can black beans, drained and rinsed
2 medium tomatoes, minced
2 long green chile peppers, roasted, peeled, and chopped
1 cup chopped red onion
2 green onions, chopped
3 tablespoons chopped fresh cilantro
1 clove garlic, peeled and minced
1 tablespoon olive oil
Juice of 1 lime
Salt
Pepper

Remove kernels from ear of corn, and combine with remaining ingredients in a bowl. Stir well.

Buy Me Some Peanuts and ... Sushi?

Peanuts, Cracker Jacks, and hot dogs used to be about the only foods sold at ballparks, but not anymore—diet- and health-conscious fans have created a market for more innovative offerings. So next time you go to a ballpark, you might hear a vendor shout, "Clam chowder, calamari, wine!" or "Get your plantains here!"

When members of the American Dietetic Association recently visited professional ballparks around the country, here's what they found:

–They could buy hot dogs, peanuts, nachos, ice cream, popcorn, pretzels, beer, and soft drinks at every ballpark they visited.

–They could buy bottled water, pizza, burgers, and candy at almost every ballpark.

–They found that 22 Major League parks offer grilled or baked chicken sandwiches and 5 serve veggie burgers.

–They found frozen yogurt available at 21 parks.

If you're in the mood for something even more exotic, visit one of these innovative stadiums:

–Oriole Park at Baltimore's Camden Yards offers crab cakes and Polynesian hot dogs.

Photograph courtesy of National Baseball Hall of Fame Library, Cooperstown, New York

Photograph courtesy of National Baseball Hall of Fame Library, Cooperstown, New York (copyright unknown)

—Edison Field, home of the Anaheim Angels, serves a "California Roll," complete with sushi, crab, avocado, sesame, seaweed, ginger paste, and hot mustard.

—San Francisco's 3 Com Park serves clam chowder in sourdough bowls as well as calamari, yellowfin tuna sandwiches, and California wines.

—Atlanta's Turner Field celebrates local cuisine by serving up Georgia pecans, Georgia Peaches-and-Cream frozen yogurt, and Cobb Salad. The park also boasts a "Taste of the Majors" concession stand that offers the regional cuisine of the visiting team. For example, when the Phillies are in town, fans can sample a Philly cheesesteak.

—Miami's ProPlayer Stadium menu celebrates Florida's Latin influences. Fans can sample *arepas* (South American cornmeal crepes with cheese), rice and beans, media noche (midnight sandwich made with a sweet bread, roast pork, ham, Swiss cheese, mayonnaise, mustard, and pickles), plantains, flan, and Cuban ham croquettes.

Evidently a good number of fans still prefer the traditional ballpark foods though. *USA Today* reported that during the first 19 days of the 1994 player strike, big league teams lost revenue on estimated sales of 9,293,399 12-ounce beers, 4, 770,611 hot dogs, and 394,969 boxes of Cracker Jack.

Gene Autry

Photograph courtesy of Maxine Hansen, Executive Assistant, on behalf of Jackie and Gene Autry

S ome of you probably wonder why we include Gene Autry in a baseball cookbook. Gene and his wife, Jackie, are big baseball fans and were the principal owners of the California Angels before the team was sold to the Disney Corporation. Of course Gene is still best known as a legendary Western movie star and recording artist. Among his many credits is the holiday classic "Rudolph the Red-Nosed Reindeer," which was written and first performed by Gene.

Gene and Jackie now oversee the Gene Autry Western Heritage Museum in Los Angeles. This beautiful collection show-cases both art and memorabilia of the Old West.

Gene Autry's Texas Chili

1½ pounds lean ground round
1 clove garlic, chopped
1 medium onion, chopped
1 medium green pepper, chopped fine
1 package Chili Sauce or 1 bottle Red Devil Chile Sauce
1 (1-pound) can kidney beans
1 small can tomatoes, chopped fine
1 cup grated Jack cheese
Additional chopped fresh onion

Brown meat, garlic, onion, and green pepper in a large skillet or Dutch oven. Add Chili Sauce, kidney beans, and tomatoes; simmer over high heat for 1 hour.

Just before serving, stir in Jack cheese to thicken chili. Top each serving with chopped fresh onion.

Makes 6 servings.

The chef of the Gene Autry Dining Room sent us the recipe for this pie, which has been served on many special occasions.

Gene Autry's Peanut Butter Pie

1 cup peanut butter
1 (8-ounce) package cream cheese
1 cup sugar
2 tablespoons melted butter
1 cup heavy cream, whipped
1 tablespoon vanilla
1 graham cracker pie crust
Hot fudge sauce

Cream together peanut butter, cream cheese, and sugar. Stir in melted butter, whipped cream, and vanilla. Mix well and pour into graham cracker crust. Chill at least 4 hours or until set firm.

Top with melted, thinned hot fudge sauce; chill at least 30 minutes.

Ken Berry

Photograph courtesy of Ken Berry

Ken Berry was born in Kansas City, Missouri. From 1962 through 1975 he earned a reputation as a slick-fielding outfielder for the White Sox, Angels, Indians, and Brewers. Ken also gave a steady performance at the plate with 1,053 career base hits.

Ken led American League outfielders in fielding percentage three times and was a two-time Gold Glove winner. He once handled an incredible 510 consecutive outfield chances without a miscue.

Ken and his wife, Aleda, now reside in Topeka, Kansas.

Frosted Old-Fashioned Amaretto Brownies

2 cups sugar
1³/₄ sticks butter, melted
4 eggs, beaten
2 cups flour
¹/₄ teaspoon salt
4 tablespoons cocoa powder or 2 squares unsweetened
    baking chocolate, melted
2 tablespoons amaretto
1 cup chopped pecans (optional)
Frosting (see recipe below)

Preheat oven to 350°.

Combine sugar with melted butter; stir in eggs. Add flour, salt, cocoa, and amaretto; stir well. Stir in pecans if desired (mixture will be thick).

Spread mixture onto a greased jellyroll pan. Bake 12–15 minutes.

Frost while brownies are still warm.

Frosting

4 tablespoons butter
2 tablespoons cocoa powder
4 tablespoons hot water
2 cups powdered sugar
2 teaspoons amaretto

Melt butter in a medium saucepan over medium heat. Add cocoa powder and stir well.

Remove pan from heat, and stir in hot water. Add powdered sugar and amaretto; mix until smooth.

Frosted Peanut Butter Fingers

1¹/8 cups butter or margarine
1¹/8 cups sugar
1¹/8 cups brown sugar
2 large eggs
3/4 cup peanut butter
1¹/2 teaspoons baking soda
1¹/2 teaspoons vanilla
2¹/2 cups flour
2 cups rolled oats
Frosting (see recipe below)

Preheat oven to 350°.

Cream butter with sugars; beat in eggs. Add peanut butter, baking soda, and vanilla; mix well. Stir in flour and oats (mixture will be thick).

Spread mixture onto a greased jellyroll pan. Bake 15–20 minutes.

Frost while brownies are still warm.

Frosting

1/4 cup cocoa powder
1/2 cup peanut butter
1/4 cup milk
1¹/2 teaspoons vanilla
1³/4 cups powdered sugar

Combine all ingredients except powdered sugar in a medium saucepan. Cook over medium heat, stirring constantly, until mixture is thick and smooth.

Remove from heat and stir in powdered sugar.

Speaking about Food

Former Boston Red Sox manager Johnny Pesky once said, "When you win you eat better, sleep better, and your beer tastes better. And your wife looks like Gina Lollobrigida." Later he thoughtfully added, "My wife is PRETTIER than Gina!"

— Slugger "Boog" Powell once said, "Sometimes, when you're driving, the car just seems to turn by itself into McDonald's. And while you're there, you might as well get a large order of fries!"

— When someone asked "King" Kelly if he drank alcoholic beverages while playing, he said, "It all depends on the length of the game."

— Former Minnesota Twins All-Star Gary Gaetti said, "The thrill of playing in your first All-Star game ranks right up there with eating lobster."

— After paying nearly $50 for a lobster dinner, Ron Kittle said, "The menu listed it at market price. I didn't know it meant stock market."*

— When asked if he liked to eat snails, Rocky Bridges said, "I prefer fast foods."*

— Pitcher Tommy John said, "I'm a light eater—when it gets light, I start eating."*

— Joe Magrane said, "What I like best about baseball is the post-game spread in San Francisco."*

— After playing winter ball in the Dominican Republic, Barry Jones said, "You eat a lot of chicken because you don't know what the other meat is."*

*Reprinted from Baseball Shorts Copyright © by Glenn Liebman; used with permission by NTC/Contemporary Publishing Company, Chicago

Wade Boggs

Photograph courtesy of Ann Wright, CSMG International, on behalf of Wade Boggs

Wade Boggs was born in Omaha, Nebraska, and is one of baseball's best pure hitters. He captured numerous batting titles while playing for the Boston Red Sox, and he continues to terrorize American League pitchers as a member of the Tampa Bay Devil Rays.

Wade considers himself a very superstitious ballplayer, and he credits a steady diet of chicken for a good part of his success. "When I started getting hits after eating chicken, I naturally began eating more," says Wade. "And I'll be doggoned if my batting average didn't continue to rise. Now I eat chicken before every single game we play."

While playing for Boston, Wade published a complete book of his favorite chicken recipes, aptly titled *Fowl Tips*. It is available through Coordinated Sports Management of Northfield, Illinois. Our thanks for their cooperation in allowing us to reprint the recipes on the next page.

Lemon Chicken

2–3 pounds chicken pieces
Garlic salt
1/2 cup butter, melted
2 teaspoons dry mustard
1 1/2 cups lemon juice

Preheat oven to 400°.

Rinse chicken and pat dry; sprinkle on all sides with garlic salt, and place in a greased shallow baking pan.

Melt butter in a saucepan; stir in dry mustard and lemon juice. Baste chicken with lemon mixture.

Bake 1 hour, basting often.

George Brett introduced Wade Boggs to Cheese Chicken in 1981.

Cheese Chicken

1/2 pound ricotta cheese
4 ounces shredded mozzarella cheese
2–3 pounds chicken pieces
1/2 cup butter, melted

Preheat oven to 350°.

Combine cheeses in a small mixing bowl.

Loosen skin on chicken pieces, leaving the skin on the chicken. Spread cheese mixture under chicken skin.

Place chicken in a shallow baking dish, and baste with butter.

Bake 1 hour, basting occasionally.

Ray Boone

Photograph courtesy of Baseball Hall of Fame Library, Cooperstown, New York

The versatile Ray Boone, a California native, starred at three different positions during his 13-season career. His big break came in 1948 when an injury to Cleveland's star shortstop, Lou Boudreau, created a vacancy on the Indians' Major League roster. Ray assumed the starting role in 1950, and hit a solid .301.

In 1953 Ray was dealt to Detroit and switched to third base. He developed into an all-star performer, leading the American League with 116 runs batted in during the 1955 season.

Ray's lifetime numbers include 1,260 hits and 151 homers. His son, Bob, also played professional baseball and retired having caught in more games than any backstop in big league history to that time. Ray's grandson Bret, an infielder with Cincinnati, is the third generation of Boones to play baseball at the Major League level.

Broccoli Salad

1 head broccoli, chopped
4 ounces shelled sunflower seeds
1 small red onion, chopped
1 tomato, chopped
1 stalk celery, chopped
1/2 pound bacon, fried crisp and crumbled
1 cup mayonnaise
1/2 cup sugar
2 tablespoons cider vinegar

Combine broccoli, sunflower seeds, onion, tomato, celery, and crumbled bacon in a large salad bowl.

Combine mayonnaise, sugar, and cider vinegar; pour dressing over salad and toss well.

Jim Bouton

Photograph courtesy of Jim Bouton

Jim Bouton, who was born in 1939 in Newark, New Jersey, wrote *Ball Four*, the bestselling book that ripped the cover off the professional baseball world. Written in journal format, *Ball Four* details Jim's behind-the-scenes experiences as an over-the-hill pitcher with the expansion Seattle Pilots in 1969.

Jim was not always the washed-up, wisecracking ballplayer portrayed in his book, however. Earlier in his career he was the pitching ace of the powerful New York Yankees, winning 21 games in 1963, and playing in both the 1963 and '64 World Series. "Bulldog" was 2–0 in the '64 Series and posted a 1.48 lifetime postseason earned run average in 24 1/3 innings of work. From 1962 through 1970 Jim played for the Yankees, Houston Astros, and Pilots, and he made a brief comeback with the Atlanta Braves in 1978.

Jim is also an inventor, whose better-known creations include Big League Chew shredded bubblegum, Big League personalized baseball cards, and the Table-to-Go picnic table. He does motivational speaking and enjoys pitching in semi-pro baseball games.

The recipe Jim submitted for this book reflects his quirky sense of humor.

Army Jell-O

1 large rubber garbage can (new)
1 garden hose (attached to a faucet)
287 packages Jell-O

Fill garbage can with water using the hose. Stir in Jell-O, and let mixture sit overnight.

Makes 400 servings.

What's in a Name?

The following men have all played Major League baseball.

"Bananas" Benes
"Buttermilk" Dowd
"Brandy" Davis
"Candy" LaChance
"Catfish" Hunter
"Chicken" Hawks
"Chili" Davis
"Chops" Broskie
"Cookie" Rojas
"Cuke" Barrows
"Ginger" Shinault
"Ham" Hyatt
"Honey" Barnes
"Hot Potato" Hamlin
"Jam" Pettibone
"Lollipop" Killefer
"Mayo" Smith
"Noodles" Zupo
"Oyster" Burns
"Pea Soup" Dumont
"Peach Pie" O'Connor

"Peanuts" Lowrey
"Pepper" Martin
"Pickles" Dillhoefer
"Pie" Traynor
"Pretzels" Pezzulo
"Puddin' Head" Jones
"Punch" Knoll
"Prunes" Moolic
"Rabbit" Maranville
"Raw Meat" Rodgers
"Salty" Parker
"Soupy" Campbell
"Spinach" Melillo
"Spud" Chandler
"Sugar" Cain
"Sweetbreads" Baily
"Taffy" Wright
"Tomato Face" Lamabe
"Turkey" Tyson
"Vinegar" Bend Mizell
"Yam" Yaryan

Bobby Bragan

Photograph courtesy of Bobby Bragan

Bobby Bragan was born in Birmingham, Alabama, in 1917. He played seven seasons in the 1940s as a catcher and shortstop with the Philadelphia Phillies and Brooklyn Dodgers.

Bobby is perhaps best known to baseball fans as a colorful field manager and baseball administrator. He has managed the Pittsburgh Pirates, the Cleveland Indians, and the Milwaukee Braves. He was also the very first skipper of the Atlanta Braves.

During his managerial years the wily Bobby had many highly publicized and often comical run-ins with Major League umpires. He later served as president of both the Texas League and the National Association of Professional Baseball Leagues.

Bobby now resides in Fort Worth, Texas, where he works with the Texas Rangers in a public relations capacity. He is an accomplished singer and pianist who still loves to entertain crowds of all ages.

Alabama Rum Cake

1 package Pillsbury Butter Flavor Cake Mix
1 package French Vanilla Pudding Mix
1/2 cup rum
1/2 cup water
1/2 cup vegetable oil
4 eggs
1/2–1 cup chopped pecans
Rum Sauce (see recipe below)

Preheat oven to 350°.

Place all cake ingredients except pecans in a large bowl; beat with mixer until fluffy.

Line the bottom of a greased Bundt pan with chopped pecans. Pour cake batter into pan, and bake 45 minutes.

Pour two-thirds of the Rum Sauce over the cake while it is still in the pan. Turn cake out onto a plate and pour remaining sauce over top.

Rum Sauce

1 stick butter
1/4 cup rum
1/4 cup water
1 cup sugar

Combine all ingredients in a saucepan; cook and stir over medium heat until boiling. Remove from heat.

Harry Brecheen

Photograph courtesy of Jessie and Fred Brown on behalf of Harry Brecheen

Harry Brecheen hails from Broken Bow, Oklahoma. Known as "The Cat," Harry was one of the game's craftiest hurlers from 1940 to 1953. He spent his entire diamond career in the city of St. Louis–11 years with the Cards and 1 with the Browns. Harry racked up 132 wins and a sparkling .589 lifetime winning percentage.

"The Cat" was at his graceful best while under pressure. He was 4-1 in three World Series, with a microscopic 0.83 earned run average over 32²/₃ innings. Harry dominated National League hitters in 1948, going 20-7, while leading the circuit in strikeouts, shutouts, and earned run average.

Harry, who is now in his eighties, lives in Ada, Oklahoma. He gave us one of his family's favorite recipes for this book.

Coconut Pound Cake

5 eggs, beaten
2 cups sugar
1 cup cooking oil
2 cups flour
1¹/₂ teaspoons baking powder
¹/₂ teaspoon salt
1 teaspoon vanilla
1 teaspoon coconut flavoring
¹/₂ cup milk
7 ounces grated coconut

Preheat oven to 325°.

Combine all ingredients, and mix thoroughly. Pour cake batter into a tube pan that has been sprayed with nonstick cooking spray.

Bake for about 1 hour or until firm.

Harry Caray

Photograph courtesy of Harry Caray and WGN Television

HARRY CARAY'S
SINCE 1987
RESTAURANT

Harry Caray, a 50-year veteran announcer, was the "Voice of the Chicago Cubs" from 1982 through 1997. His famous rendition of "Take Me Out to the Ballgame" and his trademark "Holy Cow!" became traditions with baseball fans in the Windy City and beyond. Sadly, Harry passed away in February 1998. He will be greatly missed.

Born Harry Christopher Carabina in a tough section of St. Louis, Harry was orphaned at age 9 and was living on his own by 16. He landed his first radio job in Joliet, Illinois, at age 19, and when someone suggested he shorten his name, he had it legally changed to Caray. He announced his first Major League game in St. Louis in the mid-1940s and went on to work with the Oakland A's, Chicago White Sox, and his beloved "Cubbies."

Harry and his wife, "Dutchie," spent summers in Chicago and winters in Palm Springs, California. In addition to his announcing career, Harry owned Harry Caray's Restaurant, a traditional Italian steakhouse in one of Chicago's most architecturally significant buildings. The restaurant features a first-rate collection of baseball memorabilia and a bar that is 60 feet 6 inches long—the exact distance from the pitcher's mound to home plate. To make reservations customers dial H-O-L-Y-C-O-W.

Harry had a real weakness for Italian cuisine, and Steak Vesuvio is a popular choice at his restaurant. Many thanks to Chef Abraham Aguirre and Manager Debra Elmy for this primo recipe.

Steak Vesuvio

1 (23-ounce) prime porterhouse steak
1/2 teaspoon salt
1/2 teaspoon pepper
2 teaspoons oregano
2 teaspoons granulated garlic
1 large Idaho potato
6 tablespoons olive oil
2 large whole garlic cloves
2 pieces red and yellow vinegar peppers
1/2 cup dry white wine
2 ounces frozen peas, blanched*
2 teaspoons chopped parsley

To blanch peas, place them in boiling water for 1 minute; add 1 teaspoon sugar to bring out the natural sweetness.

Trim excess fat off steak, and season well with salt, pepper, oregano, and granulated garlic.

Peel potato and cut into quarters. Saute potato quarters in olive oil in a 10-inch skillet until golden brown; remove from skillet, and set aside.

Reheat the olive oil to 300° (almost boiling); add whole garlic cloves and cook for 2 minutes to release the flavor.

Add steak to the skillet, and saute lightly on both sides until golden brown; add potato quarters and pepper pieces. Deglaze the pan with wine.

Place steak on a serving platter, and arrange potato quarters and pepper pieces around it. Pour wine sauce from pan over steak; top with peas. Garnish with parsley.

Sherry Davis

Photograph courtesy of Sherry Davis

E very Major League team employs a public address voice to introduce players and make special announcements. There is something decidedly unique, however, about the voice that rings through the air at San Francisco's 3 COM Park. That voice belongs to Sherry Davis, the first female public address announcer in the Major Leagues.

Davis is now in her fifth year with the Giants. In an open audition held in 1993 she beat out hundreds of applicants for this coveted position.

Away from the ballpark, Sherry enjoys cooking at her home in Walnut Creek, California. This traditional Southern recipe is one of her favorites.

Sherry's Spoon Bread

3 cups milk (whole milk works best)
1 cup cornmeal
1 teaspoon salt
1 1/2 teaspoons sugar
2 tablespoons butter
3–5 eggs, separated
1 tablespoon baking powder

Preheat oven to 350°.

Pour milk into a medium saucepan and heat over medium heat to simmering, stirring constantly. Slowly add cornmeal while stirring. Add salt, sugar, and butter; stir over medium heat until mixture is thickened. Remove from heat and allow to cool thoroughly.

Beat egg yolks lightly with baking powder; add to cooled cornmeal mixture.

Beat egg whites until stiff (but not dry) and fold into cornmeal mixture.

Pour mixture into a greased shallow baking dish (Sherry uses a large cast-iron frying pan).

Bake for about 1 hour or until the top is golden brown. "Spoon" the bread from the pan onto serving plates.

Moe Drabowsky

Photograph courtesy of Myron Walter Drabowsky

One of a small number of Major Leaguers born in Poland, Myron Walter "Moe" Drabowsky signed with the Chicago Cubs as a 21-year-old starting pitcher in 1956. The free-spirited Moe often called out for pizza and Chinese food from the bullpen. During his 17-year Major League career Moe pitched for the Cubs, Milwaukee Braves, Cincinnati Reds, Kansas City A's, Baltimore Orioles, Kansas City Royals, St. Louis Cardinals, and Chicago White Sox.

Some fans might remember Moe as one of the heroes of the 1966 World Series. He turned in a perfect 7-0 record for the Baltimore Orioles that year, including an almost flawless Game 1 of the Fall Classic against the Los Angeles Dodgers. Moe relieved Dave McNally in the second frame and proceeded to strike out 11 Dodgers over $6^2/_3$ innings, a record for relief pitchers. Moe and the Orioles posted a 5-2 victory in that game and went on to a four-game sweep. Moe's career earned run average in World Series play (1966 and 1970) is an astonishing 0.90.

Jay Johnstone, a former ballplayer and well-known eccentric, remembers being introduced to Moe. "The first time I met him was at a restaurant in New York. A friend said, 'Jay, I'd like you to meet Moe Drabowsky.' With that Moe dropped his cocktail glass and reached out to shake my hand. I mean, it shattered all over the floor and he didn't blink an eye. I knew right away that he was my kind of guy."

Moe's wife, Rita, suggests serving Moe's Mexican Potatoes with hamburgers or baked ham.

Moe's Mexican Potatoes

1 (16-ounce) package frozen O'Brien potatoes,
   partially thawed
1 (8-ounce) jar mild Mexican Cheez Whiz
1 (10-ounce) can cream of chicken soup

Preheat oven to 350°.

Combine all ingredients in a large bowl; mix well. Spoon mixture into a glass baking dish that has been coated with cooking spray.

Bake 1 hour.

Lenny Dykstra

Photograph courtesy of Lenny Dykstra and the Philadelphia Phillies

A native of California, Lenny Dykstra earned the nickname "Nails" with his hard-nosed style of play. This scrappy 5-foot 10-inch, 160-pound outfielder has worn both Mets and Phillies uniforms and has appeared in the World Series with both clubs.

Lenny was a key member of the 1986 World Champion Mets, rapping out 8 base hits, including 2 home runs in the 7-game showdown with the Boston Red Sox. His best season at the plate came in 1990, when he hit a sizzling .325 for the Phillies with a league-leading 192 hits.

Lenny's wife, Terri, was kind enough to provide us with this Dykstra family recipe.

Broccoli-Rice Casserole

1 medium onion, chopped
1 stalk celery, chopped
1 stick butter or margarine
1 (10-ounce) box frozen chopped broccoli
1 can cream of chicken soup
8 ounces Cheez Whiz
2 cups cooked rice
Tabasco sauce
1 cup crushed Ritz crackers
2 tablespoons melted butter

Preheat oven to 350°.

Saute onion and celery in butter until wilted. Set aside.

Cook broccoli according to package directions and drain.

Add broccoli, soup, Cheez Whiz, rice, and Tabasco sauce to onion-celery mixture, and stir well. Pour mixture into a greased baking dish, and bake for 35 minutes.

Combine cracker crumbs and melted butter. Remove casserole from oven and sprinkle with buttered crumbs. Bake an additional 10 minutes or until lightly browned.

The Peanut... in a Nutshell

The bond between peanuts and baseball is so strong that a riot almost broke out during the game's early years when one ballpark banned the sale of peanuts because the shells made such a hard-to-clean-up mess. Needless to say park officials quickly withdrew their ban. Fortunately for today's stadium crews, modern blowing equipment makes cleaning up peanut shells a "breeze"!

African slaves brought peanuts to the New World from Africa, and the slang term "goober" comes from the African peanut god, Nguba. Production and consumption of peanuts in America increased during the Civil War primarily because they are inexpensive, high in protein, and stay fresh for long periods of time.

In the 1890s Dr. George Washington Carver developed more than 300 uses for the versatile peanut, including using them in ink, lipstick, paint, soap, explosives, shaving cream, shampoo, and ice cream. According to the National Peanut Council, the average U.S. citizen consumes nearly 11 pounds of peanuts each year and Americans devour enough peanut butter annually (about 800 million pounds!) to completely coat the floor of the Grand Canyon.

In addition to consuming our fair share of peanut butter-and-jelly sandwiches, my family and I enjoy homemade peanut soup, a Virginia specialty.

Gary's Peanut Soup

1 medium onion, chopped
3 stalks celery, chopped
1/3 cup butter
3 tablespoons flour
2 quarts chicken stock or canned chicken broth
1/2 cup peanuts
1 tablespoon oil
1 1/2 cups smooth peanut butter
1 3/4 cups light cream
Chopped peanuts

Saute onion and celery in butter until soft. Add flour, stirring until well blended. Gradually add chicken stock, stirring until smooth.

Bring mixture to a boil, stirring constantly. Remove from heat and strain.

Place 1/2 cup peanuts and oil in a food processor, and process until smooth. Add ground peanut mixture, peanut butter, and cream to strained mixture, stirring until well blended and smooth. Cook over low heat until warm (do not boil).

Garnish each serving with chopped peanuts.

Carl Erskine

Photograph courtesy of Carl Erskine

Carl is a Midwest native who played his entire career in Dodger Blue—10 years in Brooklyn and 2 years in Los Angeles. A diminutive pitcher with a big heart, he posted a lifetime winning percentage of .610 (122–78).

Carl put together 10 consecutive winning seasons for "The Bums." His lone 20-game campaign came in 1953, when he was 20–6. "Oisk" pitched in five World Series (all against the Yankees) and was a key member of Brooklyn's only World Championship team (1955).

Carl and his wife, Betty, make their home in Carl's hometown of Anderson, Indiana. Betty tells us that the recipe they submitted for this book is an "Indiana classic."

Three-Corn Casserole

1/2 cup butter or margarine, softened
1 cup sour cream
1 egg, beaten
1 (16-ounce) can whole-kernel corn, drained
1 (16-ounce) can cream-style corn
1 (9-ounce) package corn muffin mix

Preheat oven to 375°.

Mix butter, sour cream, and egg. Stir in remaining ingredients, and spoon mixture into a greased 2-quart casserole dish.

Bake about 1 hour.

Dizzy Dean Speaks Out on Food

In the years following his retirement from baseball, Dizzy Dean's weight ballooned from 175 to over 250 pounds. Food seemed to occupy many of Dean's thoughts—especially when he was in the broadcast booth. He was known to share a recipe for angel food cake, rave about Miss Glo's blueberry cobbler, or describe a great peach pie he'd sampled in Shreveport, Louisiana.

A classic on-the-air conversation between Dizzy and Pee Wee Reese, his broadcast partner, went something like this:

Dizzy: "I'm going out for hamburgers. Do you want one?"
Pee Wee: "Yeh. Get me one."
Dizzy: "Pickle, mustard, or lettuce?"
Pee Wee: "See if they have some onions."
Dizzy: "Can you eat two?"
Pee Wee: "One'll do."
Dizzy: "You sure?"
Pee Wee: "Yep."
Dizzy: "OK. I'll be back directly."
Pee Wee: "Let's see, folks, where were we?"

Bob Feller

Photograph courtesy of Robert Feller and the Cleveland Indians

"Rapid Robert" was born on a farm near Van Meter, Iowa, and signed with the Cleveland Indians in 1935 at the tender age of 16. The following season "Bullet Bob" established an American League record by striking out 17 Philadelphia A's in 1 game.

Bob served almost 4 years in the navy during World War II and received 8 Battle Stars for his outstanding service on the U.S.S. *Alabama.* The war years, which came while Bob was in his prime, cost him a shot at 300 career victories. He played for the Indians his entire baseball career and finished with a 266–162 record and 3 No-Hitters.

In 1962 Bob was elected to the National Baseball Hall of Fame. During Professional Baseball's Centennial Celebration in 1969 he was voted "The Greatest Living Righthanded Pitcher."

Bob and his wife, Anne, live in Gates Mill, Ohio.

Fruitcake

4½ cups seedless raisins
2 cups water
2 cups sugar
¼ cup shortening
2½ cups flour
1 teaspoon cinnamon
¼ teaspoon ground allspice
½ teaspoon ground cloves
1 teaspoon baking powder
1 teaspoon baking soda
½ teaspoon salt
2 eggs, beaten
2 cups candied fruit
1 cup walnuts

Preheat oven to 300°.

Wash raisins. Place raisins, water, and sugar in a large saucepan, and cook over medium heat for 5 minutes; add shortening. Remove from heat and let mixture cool to room temperature.

Sift together flour, spices, baking powder, baking soda, and salt. Gradually blend in the beaten eggs. Stir in the raisin mixture, candied fruit, and walnuts.

Grease a tube pan, line with waxed paper, and grease a second time. Pack fruitcake mixture into pan, and bake for 1½ hours. Turn off oven; leave fruitcake in oven an additional 10 minutes before removing.

Joe Garagiola

Photograph courtesy of Joe Garagiola

Joe Garagiola, along with his childhood friend Yogi Berra, grew up in the Little Italy section, "The Hill," of St. Louis. His Major League career began with a bang with the home town Cardinals in 1946. Joe hit a robust .316 in the World Series as St. Louis defeated the Boston Red Sox for the World Championship.

Joe played catcher for four different big league clubs over nine seasons (1946–54). He launched his broadcasting career in 1955 when he announced for the Cards.

In 1960 Garagiola showcased his trademark sense of humor in the hilarious book *Baseball Is a Funny Game* (published by Harper & Row). He later became nationally recognized as the voice of NBC's "Major League Game of the Week" (1961–88) and cohost of NBC's popular *Today Show* (1969–73).

Joe now resides in Paradise Valley, Arizona, where he continues to be one of the great ambassadors for the game of baseball. His son is a top executive with the Arizona Diamondbacks.

Risotto a la Milanese

1/2 cup butter or margarine
2 tablespoons olive oil
3 slices bacon
4 large onions, peeled and diced
8 chicken livers, chopped
1 can chopped mushrooms
1 teaspoon salt
1/2 teaspoon black pepper
5 cups uncooked risotto or other white rice
10 1/2 cups chicken broth
1/2 teaspoon ground saffron

Place butter, oil, and bacon in a skillet; heat until bacon starts to brown. Add diced onion and cook until medium brown.

Add chopped livers, mushrooms, salt, and pepper. Stir well and brown for about 5 minutes.

Add rice; stir and cook for 2 minutes.

Bring broth to a boil in a saucepan; add boiling broth to rice mixture, stir well. Lower heat, cover pan, and simmer for about 25 minutes. Stir in saffron; if the rice seems too dry, add a little more broth.

Makes about 10 generous servings.

Ned Garver

Photograph courtesy of Ned Garver

N ed Garver was born on Christmas Day 1925 in Ney, Ohio. The stocky, righthanded pitcher played 14 years in the Major Leagues with the St. Louis Browns, Detroit Tigers, Kansas City Athletics, and California Angels.

Ned racked up 129 career wins, including 20 victories for the hapless Browns in 1951. This was no small accomplishment considering that the Browns lost more than 100 games that season! Ned was rewarded with a $25,000 contract for the 1952 season, making him the highest-paid player in Browns history.

This time-tested recipe has been in Ned's family for many years.

Baked Lima Beans

1 pound dried lima beans
1 teaspoon salt
1/4 pound butter
3/4 cup brown sugar
3 teaspoons dry mustard
1 tablespoon dark molasses
1 cup sour cream

Preheat oven to 350°.

Soak beans overnight; add salt and boil 50 minutes. Drain and place beans in a casserole dish. Stir in butter and remaining ingredients, mixing well.

Bake 1 hour. Let stand for an hour before serving; serve warm.

Ted Giannoulas– The Famous San Diego Chicken

Photograph courtesy of Ted Giannoulas

No, this isn't the lastest fast-food advertisement. This Famous Chicken is the alter ego of Ted Giannoulas, a son of Greek immigrants.

Ted's side-splitting antics at baseball games and other sporting events have become legendary over the past two decades. Sometimes performing more than 250 shows per year, Ted runs around the globe like a chicken with its head . . . well you get the picture!

While attending San Diego State in 1974, Giannoulas was hired by a local radio station for just $2 an hour (a "poultry" sum) to wear a chicken costume at an Easter egg hunt. This innocent beginning led to Ted's five-year association with KGB radio, highlighted by many memorable performances at San Diego's Jack Murphy Stadium.

The Chicken flew the coop in 1979 after a legal flap with the station. All told more than 55 million people have flocked to see his act—always bringing his sponsors more cluck for the buck! The Famous Chicken continues to be the mascot character to which all others are compared.

When Ted submitted his chicken recipe for this book, he stated it "will eliminate my competition!" He suggests serving it with a green salad and crusty French bread.

Ted's Famous Chicken

2 cans cream chicken soup
2 cups sour cream
6 boneless chicken breasts, cooked and sliced
10–12 ounces spaghetti, cooked and drained
3 ($4\frac{1}{2}$-ounce) cans button mushrooms, drained
Salt
White pepper
Freshly grated Parmesan cheese

Preheat oven to 350°.

Blend soup and sour cream in a large bowl until smooth. Gently fold in sliced chicken, spaghetti, and mushrooms; season with salt and white pepper to taste.

Pour mixture into a 9 x 13-inch baking dish, and top with cheese.

Bake 30 minutes or until center bubbles.

Wayne Hagin

Photograph courtesy of Wayne Hagin

W ayne is now in his fifth year as the play-by-play voice of the Colorado Rockies. A native of Denver, Wayne is already in his fourteenth year as a Major League announcer. He has spent time behind the mike with the A's, the Giants, and the White Sox. A former collegiate player at San Diego State, Wayne was one of the original "SportsCenter" anchors for ESPN when they hit the airwaves in 1979.

Wayne and his wife, Valerie, have two children and reside in the Highlands Ranch suburb of the "Mile-High City."

Wayne suggests serving this cheesecake with sliced, fresh peaches.

Grandma Pat's Cheesecake
Crust

1²/₃ cups graham cracker crumbs
2 tablespoons sugar
2 tablespoons melted butter

Filling

1¹/₂ pounds cream cheese, softened
1 cup sugar
3 eggs
¹/₂ teaspoon vanilla

Topping

1 pint sour cream
3 tablespoons sugar
¹/₂ teaspoon vanilla

Preheat oven to 350°.

Combine all ingredients for crust and mix well. Press crust mixture into bottom and sides of a springform or tube pan.

Make filling by creaming together softened cream cheese and sugar. Beat in eggs, one at a time; stir in vanilla. Pour filling into crust and bake 30–40 minutes.

Stir together topping ingredients. Remove cake from oven and pour topping over cake.

Increase oven temperature to 500° and bake cake an additional 5 minutes.

Makes 10 to 12 servings.

Ralph Houk

Photograph courtesy of Ralph Houk

R alph Houk was born in 1919 in Lawrence, Kansas. After serving in the armed forces during World War II, Ralph spent 8 seasons (1947–54) as backup catcher for the New York Yankees. Ralph saw very little playing time as he watched Yogi Berra achieve greatness behind the plate, but he put his countless hours on the bench and in the bullpen to good use. He spent the time learning the game inside and out from one of the true masters, Casey Stengel.

Ralph served as a coach under Casey from 1958 until 1960 and then took over the reins in 1961. The Bronx Bombers won 109 games that year as Roger Maris and Mickey Mantle combined for 115 home runs. Ralph captured 3 American League pennants and 2 world championships in his first 3 seasons as the Yankees' manager.

Over a period of 20 years Houk won 1,619 games as skipper of the Yanks, Tigers, and Red Sox. He also served as vice president and general manager of the Yankees from 1964 until 1966. Not bad for a guy who never hit a big league homer!

Ralph is now enjoying retirement in Florida.

Ralph suggests serving this goulash with fruit salad and garlic bread.

Goulash

2 pounds ground chuck
1 large onion, chopped
1 green pepper, chopped
2 celery stalks, chopped
1/4 cup butter
2 (14-ounce) cans stewed tomatoes
Oregano
Salt
Pepper
Cooked noodles or rice

Cook meat in a large skillet until lightly browned.

In a separate skillet saute onion, green pepper, and celery in butter; combine with cooked meat. Add stewed tomatoes and seasonings.

Simmer on medium-low heat for about 2 hours. Serve over noodles or rice.

Larry Jansen

Photograph courtesy of Larry Jansen

Larry Jansen, a native of Verboort, Oregon, stepped into the national pitching spotlight by winning a staggering 30 games in the Pacific Coast League in 1946. A year later he enjoyed a 21–5 rookie season with the New York Giants. His lofty .808 winning percentage led all National League pitchers. In 1950 Larry had a league high 5 shutouts, and in 1951 he and Sal Maglie each won 23 games, leading the Giants to the National League pennant.

Larry retired in 1956 with 122 victories and 17 shutouts. He later served as pitching coach for the San Francisco Giants and was instrumental in the development of Hall of Famers Gaylord Perry and Juan Marichal.

Steak Cantonese

1 1/2 pounds flank steak
1/4 cup water
2 tablespoons soy sauce
1 teaspoon vinegar
1 medium garlic clove, minced
1/2 teaspoon dry mustard
1 pound fresh broccoli
2 tablespoons peanut or salad oil
1 (10 3/4-ounce) can tomato soup
1 cup green onions, sliced diagonally
1/2 cup sliced water chestnuts
1/2 cup water

Place steak in freezer for 1 hour to firm. Remove from freezer and, starting at the narrow end, thinly slice steak diagonally across the grain.

Combine 1/4 cup water with soy sauce, vinegar, garlic, and mustard. Add steak and marinate 1 hour.

Remove flowerets from broccoli and break into small pieces. Peel the stalk and cut into 1-inch-long thin strips.

Pour oil into wok or skillet; preheat at HIGH for 1 minute. Add steak and marinade; cook 5 minutes, stirring often. Push steak up the sides of the wok or skillet.

Add broccoli flowerets and strips of stalk; cook 5 minutes, stirring often.

Add remaining ingredients. Heat, stirring until done.

Makes about 6 servings.

Pumpkin Pie Cake

1/2 cup brown sugar
1/2 cup white sugar
1 large can pumpkin
1 (13-ounce) can evaporated milk
1 teaspoon cinnamon
1/2 teaspoon ginger
1/4 teaspoon ground cloves
1/2 teaspoon salt
3 eggs, beaten
1 box yellow cake mix
2 tablespoons butter, melted
3/4 cup pecans or walnuts, chopped

Preheat oven to 350°.

Combine sugars, pumpkin, evaporated milk, spices, and salt. Mix in beaten eggs, and pour into a greased 9 x 13-inch pan. Top with dry cake mix.

Dribble melted butter over top and sprinkle with chopped nuts.

Bake 45–50 minutes.

The "Hot Stove" Glossary

Have you ever noticed how many baseball slang terms relate to food?

Infielders warm up with a game of "pepper."
A throw might have some "mustard" on it.
A blazing fastball is sometimes called "cheese."
A routine fly ball is a "can of corn."
A bobbled ball is a "hot potato."
The hitter uses the "meat" of the bat to hit the ball.
A home run is often called a "tater."
A short stint in the Major Leagues is a "cup of coffee."
A showoff player is called a "hotdog."
A runner gets caught in a "pickle."
An argument is called a "rhubarb."
A doubleheader is sometimes called a "double dip."

Ferguson Jenkins

Photograph courtesy of Ferguson Jenkins and the Chicago Cubs

This 6-foot 5-inch Canadian-born hurler was certainly one of the most consistent pitchers in baseball history. Although Ferguson Jenkins never played on a pennant-winning team, he won 284 big league games and posted 6 consecutive 20-win seasons!

In addition to his excellent control on the mound, "Fergie" displayed a potent bat at the plate. In 1971 he hit .243 with 6 home runs—a remarkable feat for a pitcher. Although perhaps best remembered as a Chicago Cub, Fergie had his benchmark season in 1974 when he won 25 games for the Texas Rangers.

Fergie was elected to the National Baseball Hall of Fame in 1991. He now resides in Oklahoma.

Fergie's Bagged Pheasant

1 chicken bouillon cube dissolved in $1/2$ cup hot water
1 envelope dry onion soup mix
1 orange, peeled and cut into pieces
$1/2$ cup white wine
$1/2$ cup water
Salt
Pepper
3–4 pound pheasant, cut into pieces

Preheat oven to 250°.

Combine all ingredients except pheasant in a bowl; mix well.

Place pheasant in a cooking bag; pour in seasoning mixture. Seal bag and slow roast for 4–6 hours.

Makes 4–6 servings.

Who Put the Pop in Popcorn?

Native Americans introduced the colonists to popcorn during the first Thanksgiving feast at Plymouth, Massachusetts, and now baseball fans devour thousands of buckets of popcorn each summer.

Just how does this centuries-old treat get its pop? The secret ingredient is the plain old water inside every kernel of corn. When a kernel is heated the temperature of the water inside rises, building pressure and taking up more space. The brittle outer skin of the kernel finally gives way, and—POP!—the kernel explodes, turning the kernel inside out and leaving a soft, white puff. Pass the salt, please!

Don Kessinger

Photograph courtesy of Don Kessinger

Don Kessinger hails from Forrest City, Arkansas. This slick fielding shortstop spent 15 seasons at the big league level— 13 with the Chicago Cubs. Kessinger joined Glenn Beckert to form the Cubbie's best double-play combo since the days of Tinker to Evers to Chance.

Don was a 6-time National League All-Star and a 2-time Gold Glove winner, with nearly 2,000 lifetime hits. In 1969 he legged out 38 doubles and scored 109 runs.

Don was an All-American baseball and basketball performer at Ole Miss in 1964, and he is now employed in the athletic department of his alma mater. He was recently honored with his own plaque on the Cubs "Walk of Fame" at Wrigley Field.

Chicken Ravioli

1 hen
1 green pepper, chopped
2 medium onions, chopped
2 tablespoons butter
1 (12–ounce) package egg noodles
1 small can pimento, chopped fine
1 small can chopped mushrooms
1 pound mild cheddar cheese, cubed

Boil hen until tender; remove hen from water, reserving broth. Remove bones and cut up meat.

Saute green pepper and onions in skillet in butter.

Cook noodles in broth until done; drain. Combine noodles with chicken, onion, green pepper, pimento, and mushrooms; add cheddar cheese and mix thoroughly.

Heat in a double boiler until cheese melts.

Vern Law

Photograph courtesy of Vern Law

Vern Law, who hails from Meridian, Idaho, was the pitching ace of the 1960 World Champion Pittsburgh Pirates. Bill Mazeroski's dramatic series-winning home run got all the headlines, but without Vern the Bucs might have been sunk. "The Deacon" posted 20 wins during the 1960 season and notched 2 more in the Fall Classic against the mighty Yankees.

A lifetime Pirate, Vern won 10-plus games in nine different years for Pittsburgh. He finished his 16-season career with a total 162 victories.

Vern now lives in Provo, Utah, with his wife, VaNita. The couple has 6 children—Veldon, Vaughn, Vance, VaLynda, Verl, and Varlin.

Vern says it takes about 3 hours from start to finish to make his Homemade Dinner Rolls—but it's worth the wait!

Homemade Dinner Rolls

2 cups warm water
3 eggs, slightly beaten
1/2 cup cooking oil
2 tablespoons dry yeast
2 teaspoons salt
1/2 cup sugar
7–8 cups flour

Combine all ingredients in a bowl, but don't handle too much! Cover bowl, and let the dough rise until double in bulk.

Punch down dough and shape into rolls; place in greased pan, cover, and let rise again.

Preheat oven to 375°.

Bake until light brown (about 8–10 minutes).

Buck Leonard

Photograph courtesy of Walter Leonard

Often referred to as the "Black Lou Gehrig," Walter F. "Buck" Leonard was one of the greatest players in the Negro Leagues of the 1930s and '40s. Buck was born in Rocky Mount, North Carolina, in 1907 and worked as a shoeshine boy and railroad yard worker before inking his first professional baseball contract at age 25.

Leonard played 17 seasons in the Negro Leagues, most of those with the legendary Homestead Grays. In his prime he was probably the third highest-paid black player, ranking behind Satchel Paige and the great Josh Gibson. But times were certainly not easy. Buck recalled getting just 60 cents a day for meal money on the road in 1934!

After the collapse of the Grays in 1950, Buck played in the Mexican League until he was 48 years old. Buck passed away at age 90 just before this book was published. A big piece of baseball history died with him.

Buck's Down-Home Macaroni and Cheese

4 ounces elbow macaroni
2 tablespoons cornstarch
1 teaspoon salt
1/4 teaspoon black pepper
1/2 teaspoon dry mustard
1 1/2 cups milk
2 tablespoons margarine
4 ounces shredded cheddar cheese

Preheat oven to 375°.

Boil macaroni 6 minutes; drain.

Combine cornstarch, salt, pepper, and dry mustard in a saucepan. Gradually add milk and cook over low heat, stirring until smooth. Add margarine, stirring constantly until mixture bubbles; boil slowly for about 1 minute.

Remove from heat and stir in almost all of the cheese, saving some for topping. Stir in cooked macaroni and turn into a greased casserole dish. Sprinkle with remaining cheese.

Bake 20 minutes or until hot and bubbly.

Makes 4 servings.

Old-Fashioned Fried Apple Rings

Apples, cored and cut into 1/4-inch rings
Flour
1 egg
1/4 cup water
Butter
Cinnamon or brown sugar

Roll apple rings in flour.

Combine egg and water. Dip floured rings in egg mixture and then roll again in flour.

Melt butter in skillet; brown rings until golden.

Sprinkle fried rings with cinnamon or brown sugar.

Mickey Lolich

Photograph courtesy of Mickey Lolich

Mickey Lolich was born in Portland, Oregon, in 1940 and became one of the true greats in Detroit Tiger history. He was the hero and Most Valuable Player in the 1968 World Series. The big lefthander posted 3 complete game wins against St. Louis in that series and outdueled Hall of Famer Bob Gibson in Game 7.

Mickey went on to become a 2-time, 20-game winner, including a league-leading 25 wins in 1971. His career totals are highlighted by 217 victories and 2,812 strikeouts. Mickey is the sole player to hit his only career home run in a World Series game.

Mickey and his wife, Joyce, operate Mickey Lolich's Donut Shop in Lake Orion, Michigan. The shop offers more than 40 varieties of doughnuts as well as a tasty assortment of cookies, muffins, and brownies. Tiger legends Jim Northrup and Kirk Gibson regularly visit Mickey's shop.

Mickey sent us two of his most popular recipes for this book.

Hello Dollies

1/2 cup butter, melted
1 cup graham cracker crumbs
1 small can grated coconut
1 small package semisweet chocolate chips
2/3 cup chopped walnuts or pecans
1 can condensed milk

Preheat oven to 350°.

Pour melted butter into the bottom of an 8 x 8-inch square pan.

Press graham cracker crumbs into bottom of pan. Sprinkle coconut evenly over crumbs; sprinkle chocolate chips and nuts over coconut. Pour condensed milk over all.

Bake 40–50 minutes or until firm.

Makes 16 squares.

Dump Cake

1 (20-ounce) can crushed pineapple
1 (20-ounce) can cherry pie filling
1 (19-ounce) package yellow cake mix
1/2 cup chopped walnuts
1/2 cup margarine

Preheat oven to 350°.

Dump pineapple and cherry pie filling into a 9 x 13-inch pan; spread yellow cake mix over top and sprinkle with nuts. Cut up margarine and place pieces on top of cake.

Bake 1 hour on lower rack of oven.

Stan Lopata

Photograph courtesy of Stan Lopata

A highly decorated World War II veteran, Michigan native Stan Lopata played 13 seasons with Philadelphia and Milwaukee and was a 2-time National League All-Star. He was the first National League catcher to wear glasses in a game.

Stan cracked 116 big-league home runs, including 32 circuit blasts for the Phillies in 1956. He hit only 21 homers in his first 6 seasons and then broke loose with 86 between 1954 and 1957.

This power outburst was due in part to some hitting advice Stan received from the legendary Rogers Hornsby. Rogers suggested a batting stance with an exaggerated crouch, and Stan's batting average immediately soared. Stan's only World Series appearance came in 1950 against the Yankees.

Stan is now retired and lives in Mesa, Arizona.

Caesar Salad

Juice of 2 lemons
1/2 cup olive oil
1/4 cup white wine vinegar
1 tablespoon Worcestershire sauce
2 whole garlic cloves, peeled
2 cups (1/2-inch) bread cubes
1/2 cup butter
2 garlic cloves, peeled and crushed
4 bunches crisp romaine lettuce
2 eggs
1/4 cup grated Parmesan cheese
1 small can anchovy fillets, diced
Salt
Freshly ground coarse black pepper

Combine first 5 ingredients and let stand several hours. Remove garlic cloves from olive oil mixture.

Toast bread cubes. Melt butter in a large pan and add crushed garlic; add toasted bread cubes, stirring until cubes absorb butter. Remove bread cubes from garlic-butter mixture.

Tear up lettuce into a large salad bowl. Break eggs over lettuce; add olive oil mixture. Toss well until traces of egg disappear.

Add cheese, anchovy, and toasted bread cubes. Add salt to taste, and pepper generously; toss well to mix.

Makes 12 servings.

Grilled Barbecued Snapper

1 small onion, chopped
1 garlic clove, minced
1/2 stalk celery, chopped
1/4 cup butter
1/2 cup ketchup
1/2 cup water
2 tablespoons lemon juice
2 tablespoons white vinegar
1 tablespoon brown sugar
1 teaspoon Worcestershire sauce
1 1/2 pounds Pacific snapper or perch fillets

Saute onion, garlic, and celery in butter. Remove from heat and add remaining ingredients except fish; stir well to blend flavors.

Rinse snapper in water and pat dry. Place in a well-greased, hinged wire fish grill.*

Baste one side of fish with sauce. Grill (basted side to the fire) about 4–6 inches from hot coals for 5–8 minutes.

Baste top with sauce. Turn and grill 7–10 minutes more or until fish flakes easily when tested with a fork.

*Stan says heavy-duty aluminum foil can be used in place of a hinged wire grill. Simply place fish on foil; baste both sides with sauce and fold edges to seal. Be sure to pierce the foil to allow smoke to enter foil and flavor the fish. Cook according to the grilling instructions above.

Hot Dog!

Photograph courtesy of National Baseball Hall of Fame Library, Cooperstown, New York

According to Oscar Meyer, the company that produces about 12.8 percent of the hot dogs on the market with machines capable of producing 38,000 frankfurters per hour, the desired meats are ground fine and then mixed with a variety of spices and curing ingredients. The mixture is "shot" into long cellulose casings that are linked or clipped into the desired "hot dog" size.

The encased hot dogs go to the smokehouse, where they are cooked. After being rinsed in cool water, the casing is peeled away before the fully cooked hot dog is packaged for sale.

The Louisville Slugger Family

L ouisville Slugger, the "Cadillac of Baseball Bats," turned 114 years old in 1998. John Andrew "Bud" Hillerich made the very first bat at his father's wood-turning business at the request of Pete "The Old Gladiator" Browning, a Louisville native and one of the greatest hitters of his era.

The rest is history. The Hillerich and Bradsby Company, based in Louisville, Kentucky, went on to become the world's leading manufacturer of baseball bats, now producing nearly 2.5 million bats annually.

The following recipe came from the fourth generation of Hillerichs, John A. Hillerich IV, and his wife, Kim.

Sweet Potato Cake

3 cups bleached flour
1 teaspoon allspice
1 cup dark brown sugar
1 can sweetened coconut
2 cups sugar
1 cup walnuts or pecans, coarsely chopped
1 can crushed pineapple
1¹/₂ cups corn oil
1 can mashed yams
4 eggs
1 teaspoon baking powder
1 teaspoon vanilla
1 teaspoon cinnamon
¹/₂ cup raisins
Icing (see recipe below)

Preheat oven to 350°.

Combine all ingredients in a large mixing bowl. Stir until combined and dry ingredients are moistened. Pour batter into 3 greased and floured 8-inch round cake pans.

Bake 30–35 minutes. Let cool 20 minutes before removing from pans; let cool to touch on racks.

Spread with icing.

Icing

1 stick unsalted butter
1 box confectioners sugar
12 ounces cream cheese, at room temperature
1 teaspoon vanilla

Cut butter into sugar. Add cream cheese and vanilla, and mix until smooth.

Ash logs from northern Pennsylvania and southern New York are brought to the Hillerich & Bradsby (H & B) mills where they are turned into "billets." The billets are sent to Louisville, Kentucky, where they are transformed into Louisville Slugger baseball bats. The following recipe comes from the kitchen of Joe and Ora Green, saw operators at the H & B mill in Ellicottville, New York. What better way to start a mill-worker's day than with a heaping stack of these hearty pancakes? The Greens suggest serving them with melted butter and real maple syrup.

Oatmeal-Banana Pancakes

1/3 cup margarine
1 1/2 cups skim milk
1 1/2 cups quick-cooking oatmeal, uncooked
1/3 cup flour
1 1/2 teaspoons baking powder
1/2 teaspoon salt
1 tablespoon sugar
1/4 teaspoon cinnamon
2 eggs, separated
2 bananas, peeled and sliced

Heat margarine and skim milk in saucepan. Stir in oatmeal and let cool.

Combine flour, baking powder, salt, sugar, and cinnamon in a bowl.

Blend egg yolks into oatmeal mixture. Stir in flour mixture.

Beat egg whites until stiff. Add whites and bananas to oatmeal-flour mixture and mix well.

Pour 1/4-cup portions of batter on a hot, lightly greased griddle. Cook pancakes until bubbles appear; turn and finish cooking.

A nother Louisville tradition is the Kentucky Derby. This festive annual event brings many things to mind, including beautiful racehorses, fancy parties, and of course food! The most famous food of all on Derby day is "Derby Pie." Louisville Slugger buyer Martha Luckett sent us her version of this time-tested classic.

First-Saturday-in-May Pie

1 cup sugar
1/4 cup flour
2 teaspoons cocoa
2 eggs, slightly beaten
1/4 pound margarine, melted and slightly cooled
1 cup pecans, broken
1 (6-ounce) package semisweet chocolate chips
1 teaspoon vanilla
1 teaspoon bourbon
1 frozen (9-inch) pie crust
Whipped cream or vanilla ice cream.

Preheat oven to 325°.

Combine sugar, flour, and cocoa. Add eggs, margarine, pecans, chocolate chips, vanilla, and bourbon; mix well.

Pour mixture into pie crust. Bake 40–45 minutes.

Serve with whipped cream or vanilla ice cream.

Kentuckians frequently serve burgoo, a thick stew that was created especially for picnics and other outdoor gatherings. Janice Lee Isaacs, of Hillerich & Bradsby, sent us her version of this traditional dish. She says the flavor improves with standing.

Kentucky Burgoo

2 pounds beef, cubed
Soup bone
1/2 pound lamb, cubed
1 frying chicken, cut up
4 quarts water
Salt
Black pepper
Red pepper
2 cups diced potato
3 cups chopped onion
2 cups lima beans
4 carrots, diced
2 green peppers, diced
3 cups corn kernels (fresh, if available)
2 cups diced okra
6 cups diced tomato
1/2 teaspoon minced garlic
1 cup minced parsley

Combine beef, soup bone, lamb, chicken, water, salt, black pepper, and red pepper in a heavy pot with a tight-fitting lid. Bring to a boil, reduce heat, and simmer, covered, 2 hours.

Remove chicken from pot; remove skin and bones and cut meat into bite-size pieces. Return chicken pieces to pot and add potato, onion, lima beans, carrots, green peppers, and corn kernels; simmer 2 hours. Mixture will be thick, but it should not stick to the pot; add water sparingly if necessary.

Add okra, tomatoes, and garlic; simmer 1 1/2 hours. Add parsley, and remove from heat.

Makes 10 servings.

The Brown Hotel, one of the oldest hotels in Louisville, created this recipe, which is considered by some to be "the only Hot Brown"! Many Hillerich & Bradsby employees swear by this dish.

Hot Brown

4 ounces butter
About 6 tablespoons flour
3–3 1/2 cups milk
6 tablespoons grated Parmesan cheese
1 beaten egg
1 ounce whipped cream (optional)
Salt
Pepper
8–12 slices toast
Roast turkey slices
Additional Parmesan cheese
8–12 strips bacon, fried crisp

Melt butter and add enough flour to make a reasonably thick roux (enough to absorb all of the butter).

Add milk and 6 tablespoons Parmesan cheese. Add egg to thicken sauce, but do not allow sauce to boil; remove from heat.

Fold in whipped cream if desired; season with salt and pepper.

For each Hot Brown, place two slices of toast on a metal or other flameproof dish. Cover toast with liberal amount of turkey; pour generous amount of sauce over turkey and toast. Sprinkle with Parmesan cheese.

Broil until sauce is speckled brown and bubbly. Remove from broiler, cross 2 pieces bacon on top, and serve immediately.

Makes 4–6 servings.

Greg Luzinski

Photograph courtesy of Greg Luzinski

Greg Luzinski, a native of Chicago, was known as "The Bull" during his playing days ... and with good reason! The 6-foot 1-inch, 220-pound Luzinski blasted 307 home runs during his 15 seasons in the Major Leagues.

Greg spent a major part of his career in the "City of Brotherly Love" as a first baseman and outfielder for the Philadelphia Phillies. He teamed with Hall of Fame third baseman Mike Schmidt to form a powerful 1–2 punch at the plate. Greg led the National League with 120 runs batted in during 1975. His best statistical season came two years later in 1977 when he batted .309, with 39 home runs and 130 runs batted in.

Greg was also a member of the outstanding Phillies club that defeated the Kansas City Royals in the 1980 World Series. He was later swapped to the Chicago White Sox and closed out his lengthy career as a productive American League designated hitter, clubbing 32 home runs, with 95 runs batted in during the 1983 season.

"The Bull's" Brownies

1 package German Chocolate Cake Mix
3/4 cup melted margarine
1/3 cup evaporated milk
10 ounces caramel candies
1/3 cup evaporated milk
Chocolate chips

Preheat oven to 350°.

Combine cake mix, margarine, and 1/3 cup evaporated milk; stir well. Press half of mixture into a baking pan; and bake 12 minutes.

Combine caramels and remaining 1/3 cup evaporated milk; microwave or cook in a saucepan over low heat until caramels melt.

Cover baked brownies evenly with chocolate chips and caramel mixture. Crumble remaining cake mixture over top, and return to oven for 15 minutes.

Let cool completely before cutting into squares.

Mickey Mantle

Photograph courtesy of Kingdon Knowles

Regarded as the most powerful switch-hitter of all time, Mickey Mantle spent his entire Major League career in the pinstripes of the New York Yankees. Born in Oklahoma "The Mick" was named after Hall of Fame catcher Mickey Cochrane.

Mickey won the American League Triple Crown in 1956 and the League's coveted Most Valuable Player award in 1956, '57, and '62. During his glorious career Mickey played in a staggering 20 All-Star games and 12 World Series. His 18 lifetime Fall Classic homers still stand as a record. Mickey was unanimously elected to the Hall of Fame in 1974.

Mickey possessed tremendous athletic ability and blazing speed, but nagging knee injuries slowed him in his later years. He died in 1995 after a courageous battle against cancer.

Mickey Mantle has been an inspiration to millions, and a real-life hero to baseball fans worldwide. This recipe was contributed by Kingdon Knowles, the general manager of Mickey Mantle's Restaurant and Sports Bar located near New York's Central Park.

Yankee Garlic Bread

1 loaf fresh Italian or French bread
3 tablespoons unsalted sweet cream butter
   at room temperature
1 teaspoon olive oil
3–4 large cloves of garlic, finely chopped
1 shallot clove, finely chopped
3 tablespoons Parmesan cheese
1 teaspoon freshly ground black pepper
1/4 cup finely chopped parsley

Preheat oven to 425°.

Cut bread diagonally into 3/4 to 1-inch-thick slices; place on baking sheet.

Combine butter, olive oil, garlic, shallot, Parmesan cheese, and black pepper in a small bowl; mix with a fork until well blended. Spread butter mixture lightly and evenly over the top of each bread slice.

Place baking sheet on the middle rack of the oven, and bake for 6–9 minutes or until the edges of bread turn golden brown. Remove baking sheet from oven and lightly sprinkle parsley over hot bread. Serve warm.

Willie Mays

Photograph courtesy of National Hall of Fame Library, Cooperstown, New York

The "Say Hey Kid," who was born in Westfield, Alabama, in 1931, is without doubt one of baseball's true greats. Willie clubbed 660 home runs during his 22-year Major League career, including 40 or more in 6 different seasons. Many consider Mays the best all-around performer baseball has ever known.

Actress Tallulah Bankhead once said, "There were only two geniuses in the world: Willie Shakespeare and Willie Mays." Mays was inducted into the National Baseball Hall of Fame in 1979. Shakespeare is still waiting!

Willie lives in Atherton, California. This recipe from his family is featured in the highly recommended *Black Family Reunion Cookbook* available from Fireside Books.

"Say Hey" Bran Muffins

1 tablespoon baking powder
3 tablespoons natural honey
1 cup skim milk
2 eggs
1 cup natural bran
1 cup whole-wheat flour
$1/2$ teaspoon salt
Favorite fruit, if desired

Preheat oven to 350°.

Grease 12 medium ($2^{1/2}$-inch) muffin cups.

Combine all ingredients in a large bowl; stir just until blended. Fold in favorite fruit, if desired. Spoon mixture into muffin cups.

Bake 20–25 minutes.

Makes 12 muffins.

Lindy McDaniel

Photograph courtesy of Lindy McDaniel and the New York Yankees

This 6-foot 3-inch Oklahoma native recorded 141 wins and 172 saves during his 21-year Major League career. Lindy McDaniel's 119 relief victories placed him second on the all-time list behind the great Hoyt Wilhelm.

Lindy began his career as a starter with the St. Louis Cardinals, going 15-9 in 1957. He became a relief specialist in 1959 and went on to lead the National League in saves 3 times (1959, 1960, and 1963). Lindy was named to the National League All-Star team in 1960. He retired in 1975 after pitching in a total of 987 big league games for 5 different teams.

Lindy and his wife, Alice, live in Selma, California. They sent us the recipe for one of Lindy's favorite desserts.

Lindy's Homemade Ice Cream

2 eggs, beaten
2 cups milk
3/4 cup sugar
1/8 teaspoon salt
1 tablespoon vanilla
2 cups half-and-half

Combine eggs, milk, sugar, and salt in a large (to allow for foaming) microwave-safe container; stir well. Microwave mixture at HIGH for 11 minutes; let cool.

Stir in vanilla and half-and-half. Pour mixture into an ice-cream freezer; freeze. Let ice cream sit in freezer an extra hour or two to let the flavor "ripen."

Makes 1/2 gallon; double the recipe to make 1 gallon.

Strawberry Ice Cream

Make ice cream using recipe above omitting the vanilla.

Combine 1 pint fresh strawberries, sliced, with 1/4 cup sugar, and let sit 30 minutes. Add strawberries to freezer when ice cream begins to thicken.

Butter Pecan Ice Cream

Make ice cream using recipe above substituting 1 cup brown sugar for 3/4 cup sugar.

Toast 1/2 cup or more pecans in 2 tablespoons butter over low heat 5 minutes; let cool. Add toasted pecans to freezer when ice cream begins to thicken.

Peach Ice Cream

Make ice cream using recipe above.

Add 1 1/2 cups fresh peaches, peeled and chopped, to freezer when the ice cream begins to thicken.

Roy McMillan

Photograph courtesy of Roy McMillan

Texas native Roy McMillan is a 3-time Gold Glove winner who spent 16 years playing in the Major Leagues. This durable shortstop played in 584 consecutive games for Cincinnati in the early 1950s.

Roy was named a National League All-Star in 1956 and 1957. He collected 1,639 hits during his career with the Reds, Braves, and Mets. Roy also served briefly as manager of the Brewers in 1972 and the Mets in 1975.

Roy says this beef brisket recipe is very popular in his native Texas. The marinade is also good with venison.

Beef Brisket

1 tablespoon sugar
1 small bottle soy sauce
1 tablespoon Worcestershire sauce
2 tablespoons liquid smoke
1 tablespoon vinegar
1 teaspoon garlic powder
Beef brisket

Combine all ingredients except beef and mix well.

Place trimmed brisket in a pan lined with heavy-duty foil, leaving foil long enough to cover the entire brisket. Pour marinade over brisket and fold foil over top; seal foil. Refrigerate 24 hours.

Preheat oven to 250°.

Remove pan from refrigerator and immediately place in preheated oven; bake for about 4 hours or longer for a very large brisket.

Good Potatoes

1 large package frozen hash brown potatoes, thawed
1/2 cup melted butter
1 teaspoon salt
1/4 teaspoon pepper
1/2 cup chopped onion
1 can cream of chicken soup
1 (8-ounce) carton sour cream
10 ounces grated American cheese
2 cups cornflakes, crushed
1/4 cup melted butter

Preheat oven to 350°.

Combine potatoes, 1/2 cup melted butter, salt, pepper, chopped onion, chicken soup, sour cream, and American cheese. Pour mixture into a greased casserole dish.

Mix crushed cornflakes and 1/4 cup melted butter; sprinkle over top of potatoes.

Bake 45 minutes.

Makes 12 servings.

Hey, Beer Man!

In the 1880s Chris Von Der Ahe purchased the St. Louis Browns professional baseball club solely to secure the right to sell beer at Sportsman's Park. Through the years selling beer has added to the profitability of most professional teams, especially at the Minor League level, where beer may account for up to 50 percent of the gross concessions-generated income.

People have been drinking beer for more than 6,000 years, with most ancient cultures independently discovering the fermented brew. The rise of commerce and the growth of cities during the Middle Ages made beer-making more than a leisure activity, and by the twelfth-century Germans had established large-scale brewing businesses. Europeans brought beer to the New World, and the first American brewery was founded in 1623. Many of our forefathers (Thomas Jefferson, George Washington, and Samuel Adams, to name a few) developed a serious interest in making (and drinking!) beer.

As fate would have it, America's most successful commercial brewery and professional baseball took root the same year. In 1869 a 30-year-old German immigrant named Adolphus Busch purchased half-ownership of the Bavarian Brewery of St. Louis. The company was soon restructured, with Busch's father-in-law, Eberhard Anheuser, as president. Ten years later the company took the name Anheuser-Busch Brewing Association.

Through innovations such as the use of pasteurization and a network of railside icehouses, Busch was able to promote and market beer far and wide, including ballparks. The year 1993 marked the fortieth anniversary of Anheuser-Busch's purchase of the St. Louis Cardinals. Over 70 million fans have attended events at Busch Stadium since its turnstiles first swung open in 1966.

The Milwaukee Brewers went one step further in baseball's close business relationship with beer when they made Bernie Brewer one of their family in 1973. According to the club's public relations department, the front office introduced Bernie to make home games more exciting and draw bigger crowds during the team's early years.

Bernie resided in an 11-foot-tall, 12-foot-square "beer barrel" in the centerfield bleachers at County Stadium, where he led cheers from his perch. Every time the home team hit a homer or won a game, the bubbly mascot slid down a 27-foot-long steel board into an oversize suds-filled stein—all to the tune of "Roll Out the Barrel!" The fans loved it, especially when home run sluggers George Scott, Larry Hisle, and Gorman Thomas kept Bernie "on a roll."

The fun ended for Bernie and the Brewers fans in 1984 when the stadium was renovated and the chalet demolished. It took 10 years, but persistent public pressure prompted Bernie's return to his rightful place in 1993. Polka-singing fans welcomed their beloved Bernie back to his new, improved living quarters, and he has been happily sliding down into the suds ever since.

Hal McRae

Photograph courtesy of Hal McRae and the Kansas City Royals

Hal McRae, a native of Avon Park, Florida, is best remembered as a solid hitter and fiery competitor. He was a member of some great teams in Cincinnati and Kansas City and was certainly no stranger to post-season play.

Hal was at his consistent best with the Royals in the mid-1970s. In 1977 he banged out 54 doubles, 21 homers, and 92 runs batted in. Hal led the American League with 133 runs batted in during the 1982 season and was named the American League's top designated hitter five times.

Hal remains active in professional baseball in a coaching capacity. His son, big league outfielder Brian McRae, is an exciting performer in his own right.

Mac's Favorite Swiss Steak

1 large round steak
Salt
Pepper
Flour
2 tablespoons cooking oil
1 large onion, chopped
1 large green bell pepper, chopped
1/4 cup chopped celery
1/4–1/2 cup red wine
1 cup beef bouillon
1 cup water
1 (16-ounce) can tomatoes
1 (16-ounce) can sliced mushrooms, drained
Cooked rice, noodles, or potatoes

Cut steak into serving-size pieces; season with salt and pepper and coat with flour. Brown steak in large skillet in cooking oil.

Remove steak from skillet and add onion, bell pepper, and celery; saute.

Stir in red wine. Add beef bouillon, water, tomatoes, and mushrooms; bring to a boil. Add steak and simmer 45–60 minutes, stirring occasionally; add more water if necessary.

Serve over rice, noodles, or potatoes.

Makes 6–8 servings.

Minnie Minoso

Photograph courtesy of Minnie Minoso and the Chicago White Sox

Minnie Minoso was born Saturnino Orestes Armas Minoso in Havana, Cuba, in 1922. He played briefly with the Negro League New York Cubans before joining the Cleveland Indians in 1949. Minoso became Chicago's first black big leaguer just 2 years later when he was dealt to the White Sox.

Minnie's 17-year Major League career spanned 5 decades (1940–80), an all-time record. He even had an at-bat with the independent Northern League in 1993!

The fleet-footed Minoso was a 6-time American League All-Star and a Gold Glove-winning outfielder. He led the American League in triples and stolen bases 3 times while amassing 1,963 career base hits.

Minnie currently works with the White Sox community relations department, making countless personal appearances each year in the Chicago area. He recently completed his auto-biography, *Just Call Me Minnie.*

Minnie's Cuban Paella

12 clams in the shell
6 cups water
2 1/2 pounds fresh shrimp
1/4 teaspoon ground red pepper
4 tablespoons olive oil, divided
1 tablespoon butter
1 cup white rice
1 teaspoon salt
1 bay leaf
1 cube chicken bouillon
2 cloves garlic, peeled and minced
2 onions, finely chopped
2 green bell peppers, finely chopped
2 tomatoes, peeled
1/4 cup sliced black olives
1 1/2 cups cheddar cheese, finely grated

Place clams in 6 cups water and bring to a boil. Add shrimp and red pepper; boil 5 minutes. Drain; reserving 2 1/2 cups stock.

Heat 2 tablespoons oil and 1 tablespoon butter in a 3-quart saucepan. Add rice and reserved stock; stir well. Add salt, bay leaf, and bouillon cube; simmer 25 minutes.

Preheat oven to 375°.

Pour remaining 2 tablespoons oil into a 6-quart Dutch oven. Add garlic, onion, and green pepper; saute 10 minutes.

Add cooked shrimp, clams, and rice mixture along with tomatoes and olives; stir to blend. Pour all ingredients into a Paella pan or oven-safe serving dish. Sprinkle with grated cheese and bake 10–15 minutes.

Let cool 10 minutes before serving.

Makes 6–8 servings.

Morganna – The Kissing Bandit

Photograph courtesy of Morganna

The buxom Morganna began her career in Cincinnati, Ohio, at age 15, when she won a $5 bet by leaping from the stands and kissing All-Time Hit King Pete Rose. Since that first infamous kiss, Morganna has worked ballparks across the country, smooching Dodger heartthrob Steve Garvey as well as Nolan Ryan, Cal Ripken Jr., George Brett, and many other unsuspecting "victims."

Morganna's act almost always produces big laughs and at least one red-faced ballplayer, and it has taken her to jail at least 19 times. Not surprisingly Hooters often sponsors Morganna's appearances. "I may have the body of a sex symbol," says Morganna, "but I have the heart of a comedienne."

Morganna hails from Columbus, Ohio, where she enjoys this local favorite dish at Marzetti's Restaurant. The recipe was created in the 1920s and is named after the owner's brother.

Johnny Marzetti

1½ pounds ground beef
1 large onion, chopped
1 can tomatoes
1 can sliced mushrooms
1 large can tomato paste
¼ pound cheddar or mozzarella cheese, shredded
1 package egg noodles, cooked
Additional shredded cheese
Breadcrumbs

Preheat oven to 300°.

Place ground beef and onion in a large skillet; cook until browned. Add tomatoes, mushrooms, tomato paste, and ¼ pound cheese; cook over low heat, stirring frequently until well blended.

Place cooked noodles in baking pan, and top with ground beef mixture. Sprinkle with additional cheese and breadcrumbs.

Bake about 40 minutes.

Makes 8 servings.

Hal Newhouser

Photograph courtesy of the National Baseball Hall of Fame (copyright unknown)

"Prince Hal" Newhouser is a native of Detroit, Michigan, and spent the vast majority of his baseball career in the "Motor City." A fine lefthanded pitcher, Hal piled up 207 wins over 17 seasons of Major League play. He also notched two victories in the 1945 World Series when the Tigers roared past the Chicago Cubs in 7 games.

From 1944 to '46 Hal was the most dominant hurler in all of professional baseball. He posted 80 wins during those three seasons while averaging just 9 losses per year. Hal was the American League Strikeout Leader in 1944 and 1945 and the league's Earned Run Average Champion in 1945 and 1946.

Hal and his wife now reside in Bloomfield Hills, Michigan.

Potato Pancakes

2 eggs
1½ tablespoons salt
Pinch of baking powder
1 tablespoon flour
1 small onion, grated
2 cups grated potatoes
Applesauce or sour cream

Beat eggs with salt, baking powder, flour, and grated onion. Add grated potato and mix well.

Drop by large spoonfuls into a hot greased skillet. Cook until crisp and brown on both sides.

Serve with applesauce or sour cream.

Jim Northrup

Photograph courtesy of Jim Northrup

Michigan native Jim Northrup rapped out 1,254 hits during his 12-year career, hitting more than 20 home runs in three consecutive seasons (1968–70). A great hitter in the clutch, Jim once blasted 3 grand slams in a single week (a Major League record).

Jim drove in a career high 90 runs in 1968 and followed that up with a stellar performance in the World Series. He collected 2 homers and 8 runs batted in during the Tigers' 7-game triumph over Bob Gibson and the Cardinals.

He spent 10 seasons in the outfield of the Detroit Tigers. He was traded twice in 1974 and retired 1 year later.

Jim currently works as a manufacturer's representative in Southfield, Michigan.

Fettuccine with Smoked Salmon and Caviar

3 tablespoons margarine
1 medium onion, chopped
8 ounces mushrooms, sliced
2 cups milk, divided
1 tablespoon cornstarch
8 ounces smoked salmon, broken into bite-size chunks
1 pound fettuccine, cooked according to package
    instructions
Salt
Pepper
Black caviar
Chopped green onions
Grated Parmesan cheese

Melt margarine in a large skillet. Add chopped onion and saute until translucent or golden brown. Add mushrooms and cook for another minute.

Combine 1/4 cup milk and cornstarch in a small bowl.

Add remaining 1 3/4 cups milk to skillet; bring mixture to a boil over medium heat. Lower heat; add salmon and cornstarch mixture. Cook, stirring constantly, until sauce thickens.

Add cooked fettuccine, salt, and pepper; mix well.

Top each serving with 1 teaspoon caviar, 1 tablespoon green onions, and 1 tablespoon grated Parmesan cheese.

Joe Nuxhall

Photograph courtesy of Joe Nuxhall

Ohio native Joe Nuxhall is best remembered as the youngest player ever to appear in a Major League contest—he was just 15 years old when he took the mound for Cincinnati in 1944. Joe lasted less than one inning, giving up 2 hits and walking 5, but he established a record that will likely stand for many years to come.

It was nearly 8 seasons before Nuxhall would again wear a Reds uniform. Overlooked in all this trivia are Joe's 135 big league wins from 1952 to '66. He led the National League with 5 shutouts in 1955 and put together a 15-8 campaign in 1963.

Joe now shares the microphone with Marty Brennaman on Reds radio broadcasts. Ironically he is now known as "The *Old* Lefthander." Go figure!

Chicken Tortillas

6 skinned and boned chicken breasts
Salt
Pepper
Sage
6 medium-size flour tortillas
6 slices Monterey Jack cheese
1 small can whole green chiles
1 can cream of chicken soup
1/2 cup sour cream
White wine
Cheddar cheese, grated

Preheat oven to 350°.

Sprinkle chicken breasts with salt, pepper, and a little sage. Place a chicken breast on each tortilla and top with 1 slice Monterey Jack and 1 green chile. Roll up tortillas and place seam side down in a baking dish.

Mix soup and sour cream with enough wine to match the consistency of mayonnaise. Spoon over chicken rolls and bake 50 minutes.

Remove from oven and sprinkle with grated cheddar cheese; bake an additional 10 minutes.

Andy Pafko

Photograph courtesy of Andy Pafko

"Handy" Andy Pafko, one of Roger Kahn's "Boys of Summer," was born in Wisconsin in 1921. He played 17 Major League seasons as an outfielder and third baseman. Pafko starred for the Cubs, Brooklyn Dodgers, and Milwaukee Braves and appeared in the World Series for all 3 clubs. Andy's teammates included Jackie Robinson, Duke Snider, and a young Henry Aaron.

A lifetime .285 hitter, Andy blasted 213 career homers. He hit over 25 home runs 3 times and drove home 100-plus runs twice.

Andy now lives in Mount Prospect, Illinois.

Andy sent us one of his favorite Slovak recipes.

Chicken Paprikash With Egg Dumplings

Egg Dumplings

1 teaspoon salt
1/2 cup milk
1 egg, beaten
1 1/2 cups sifted flour

Add salt and milk to beaten egg. Stir into flour to form a smooth batter.

Drop by teaspoonfuls into boiling salted water; cover tightly and cook 15 minutes. Drain.

Chicken and Gravy

3 tablespoons butter or shortening
1 cup chopped onion
Salt
Pepper
2 pounds chicken pieces
2 cubes chicken bouillon
2 tablespoons sweet red paprika
1 pint sweet cream

Melt butter in Dutch oven. Add onion and saute until tender.

Salt and pepper chicken pieces; add to Dutch over. Cover with water; add bouillon cubes and paprika. Simmer about 1 hour or until chicken is tender. Remove chicken from Dutch oven.

Add sweet cream to Dutch oven; stir to blend. Add dumplings and chicken.

Steve Palermo

Photograph courtesy of Steve Palermo

Steve Palermo, who served as an American League umpire from 1977 until 1991, has been an a true inspiration to baseball fans everywhere. On July 6, 1991, Steve was shot in the back while coming to the aid of a robbery victim outside a Dallas restaurant. The suspects were eventually apprehended, but Steve was left partially paralyzed. Thanks to grueling physical therapy and a lot of determination, he has made remarkable progress and is now walking with the aid of canes.

Steve presently works as an agent for the Major League Baseball Executive Council and has conducted studies on the excessive length of big league ball games. He has not given up his dream of calling balls and strikes again.

Steve and his wife, Debbie, live in Overland Park, Kansas.

Steve says the following recipe is great either as an appetizer or entree. He especially likes to top this dish with a grilled shish kebab of shrimp, cherry tomatoes, onion, bell peppers, and mushrooms.

Capellini with Basil Cream Sauce

1½ cups heavy cream
2 tablespoons julienned basil leaves
1 teaspoon fresh lemon juice
Pinch of salt
12 ounces capellini (angel hair pasta)

Gently boil heavy cream in a saucepan until it is reduced by half (about 10 minutes). Stir in basil, lemon juice, and salt.

Cook the pasta in plenty of boiling water until firm to the bite (about 7–10 minutes); drain. Toss with the cream sauce and serve at once.

Henry's Puffy Taco

Photograph courtesy of Bryan Behan and the San Antonio Missions Baseball Club

Without a doubt the San Antonio Missions of the Class AA Texas League have the most appetizing mascot in all professional baseball: "Henry's" Puffy Taco. This delectable fan favorite comes complete with lettuce, tomatoes, and cheese. He even has jalapeno peppers for feet! The sponsor, "Henry's," is a local Mexican restaurant.

Max Patkin

Photograph courtesy of Max Patkin

Max Patkin, "The Clown Prince of Baseball," looks more like a frog than a prince and has never appeared in a Major League box score. Yet he is one of baseball's most recognizable and beloved personalities. For more than 50 years Max traveled up to 150,000 miles a year, entertaining baseball fans with his zany antics and dance routines. His rubbery face was once described as "the world's biggest hunk of chewing gum."

Now approaching 80 years old, the man with the "jointless" body is the godfather of all ballpark performers. Max has appeared in more than 4,000 stadiums as well as in the smash motion picture *Bull Durham.*

Having just completed a book of memoirs, Max is enjoying his retirement at his home in King of Prussia, Pennsylvania. "I'll take it easy, play some gin rummy, and laugh a little bit," said Max. Yes, and all of us will laugh a little bit less.

We miss ya, Max!

Max says, "This is not a family recipe. I just like it." He suggests serving the lamb chops with baked potato or thin French fries.

Max's Favorite Lamb Chops

Lamb chops
Salt
Pepper
Minced fresh garlic
Sauteed mushrooms
Fresh parsley

Preheat broiler.

Trim the outer skins of the chops, which are often strong in flavor, and season to taste with salt, pepper, and garlic. Brown chops on both sides under the broiler before cooking to desired doneness. (Max prefers his medium.)

Top with sauteed mushrooms and garnish with fresh parsley.

Boog Powell

Photograph courtesy of John Powell and Herb Allen

John "Boog" Powell was born in Lakeland, Florida. The burly Powell swatted 339 home runs over his 17-year Major League career. He was an institution as the Baltimore Orioles' slugging first baseman from 1961 until 1974, and today his barbeque stand at the beautiful new Oriole Park at Camden Yards has also become an institution.

Boog's culinary career took root in the backyard of his Baltimore rowhouse, where he hosted summer cookouts for teammates and friends. These shindigs would often take place after night games and continue into the wee hours of morning. "I'd put the food on the grill around 12:30," Boog recalls. "We'd be outside eating at 2 a.m. or later." The neighbors were either very understanding or slightly intimidated by Powell's powerful physique!

Boog is the author of *Mesquite Cookery*, a cookbook that is considered a classic among backyard chefs.

Boog's Ribs 'n' Beer Marinade

1 quart beer
2 cups brown sugar
1 cup apple cider vinegar
1 teaspoon dry mustard
2 teaspoons crushed red pepper
1 tablespoon chili powder
1 teaspoon ground cumin
2 bay leaves
6 (1½-pound) slabs pork baby back ribs
½ cup ketchup

Combine beer, sugar, vinegar, mustard, spices, and bay leaves in a large saucepan. Bring to a boil; remove from heat and let cool.

Place ribs in a large shallow roasting pan. Pour marinade over ribs and marinate 24 hours, turning ribs several times. Drain ribs and reserve marinade.

Arrange ribs on a grill or rib rack and cook 2–3 hours, or cook in a smoker 6–7 hours, until meat is tender, basting with the marinade every 20–30 minutes. When the meat is tender, brush with a little ketchup.

Makes 6–8 servings.

Boog's Steak Gaucho

1/2 pound butter
2 cups finely chopped scallions
  or 1 1/2 cups finely chopped onion
1/2 teaspoon dried rosemary, crumbled
1/2 teaspoon oregano leaves, crumbled
1 cup dry white wine
1/2 cup wine vinegar or cider vinegar
1 1/2 teaspoons salt
1 tablespoon freshly ground pepper
2 tablespoons butter
2 (3-inch-thick, 3 1/2–4 pound) sirloin steaks

Melt 1/2 pound butter in skillet over medium heat; add scallions and saute about 10 minutes or until limp but not brown. Add rosemary, oregano, wine, vinegar, salt, and pepper. Remove from heat and add 2 tablespoons of butter.

Broil steaks over hot mesquite coals about 15 minutes on each side for rare steaks. Just before serving, warm sauce over low heat, carve steak, and pour sauce over steak slices.

Makes 6–8 servings.

"Crunch Potato Slices"

In 1853 in Saratoga Springs, New York, Commodore Cornelius Vanderbilt sent his fried potatoes back to the chef, claiming they were cut too thick. The indignant chef cut a spud into paper-thin slices, fried them to a crisp, sprinkled them with salt, and sent them back to the table. Vanderbilt loved the "crunch potato slices."

Over the past 150 years potato chips have become America's most popular snack food. According to the Snack Food Association in Alexandria, Virginia, Americans annually munch about 1.5 billion pounds of potato chips. This means that the average American consumer eats an equivalent of 96 (1-ounce) bags each year! Many of those bags, I'm sure, are devoured by hungry baseball fans both at the stadium and in front of their television sets.

Rip Repulski

Photograph courtesy of Millie Repulski

Minnesota native Eldon John "Rip" Repulski broke into the big leagues as a highly touted prospect with the St. Louis Cardinals in 1953, and his aggressive nature at the plate quickly earned him the nickname "Rip." The young Repulski responded with 15 homers and 66 runs batted in during his rookie season.

Rip continued his solid play through 1957 when he was traded to the Phillies for star slugger Del Ennis. The change of venue didn't seem to hurt—the hard-swinging Repulski blasted 21 round-trippers for Philadelphia that year.

Rip retired in 1961 with 106 career homers. He passed away in 1993 at the age of 66.

Rip's wife, Millie, sent us one of Rip's favorite recipes for this book.

Fresh Peach Pie

4–5 peaches, peeled and sliced
1 baked pie crust
1$^{1}/_{2}$ cups milk
$^{1}/_{2}$ cup sugar
2 tablespoons cornstarch
Pinch of salt
2 egg yolks, beaten
1 teaspoon vanilla
2 egg whites, beaten until stiff peaks form*

Note: Whipped heavy cream may be substituted for beaten egg whites; do not brown.

Place sliced peaches in baked pie crust.

Boil milk, sugar, cornstarch, and salt until thick, stirring constantly to avoid scorching. Add beaten egg yolks and boil 2 additional minutes. Remove from heat and stir in vanilla.

Pour filling over peaches; spread beaten egg whites over filling. Brown briefly in oven or under broiler.

The Legendary Babe Ruth

Photograph courtesy of National Baseball Hall of Fame Library, Cooperstown, New York

During the 1920s Babe Ruth's eating habits became almost as legendary as his towering home runs. Babe would often wash down a handful of hot dogs with bicarbonate of soda before a game and then indulge in a postgame "snack." One night baseball great Ty Cobb watched Babe polish off six club sandwiches, a side platter of pig knuckles, and a tall pitcher of beer!

The Babe's diet briefly caught up with him on April 6, 1925, when the Yankees were traveling by train between Knoxville, Tennessee, and Asheville, North Carolina, to play an exhibition game against the Brooklyn Dodgers. He complained of feeling under the weather during the trip, and as he made his way through the terminal the mighty Babe suddenly collapsed. His teammates carried the 230-pound home run king to a taxi, rushed him to Asheville's Battery Park Hotel, and called a doctor.

Although the doctor publicly announced that Babe was suffering from "the flu," word had already spread that he had just eaten too many hot dogs and chugged too much beer on the train ride. *The Asheville Citizen* reported that "Ruth does not observe a strict diet, and this, more than anything else, was given as a probable cause for his present illness."

Since Babe had remained behind in his hotel room under the watchful eyes of a local doctor while his teammates hammered the Dodgers and then left for New York, rumors began circulating that the "Sultan of Swat" had passed away in Asheville. Even though Babe soon recovered and rejoined the Yankees, news of his death continued to be passed around the world for some time.

Babe's infamous "Bellyache Heard 'Round the World" apparently played a key role in his lackluster performance in 1925. Without the slugger's usual contribution of game-winning homers, the Bronx Bombers ended the season in 7th place, one of the team's worst finishes of that period.

Pete Rose

Photograph courtesy of Pete Rose and the Cincinnati Reds

Pete Rose is the quintessential overachiever. While growing up in Cincinnati he dreamed of playing for his hometown Reds. Pete's God-given talents were never considered exceptional, but he loved the game and always gave 110 percent. He was dubbed "Charlie Hustle" early in his career, and that handle has stuck with him to the present.

Pete was named National League Rookie of the Year in 1963 as the Reds' second baseman. When he hung up his spikes in 1986, Pete was baseball's all-time leader in hits, singles, at-bats, and games played. He was a 16-time All-Star and played in 6 World Series (4 with the "Big Red Machine" and 2 with the Phillies). Pete is the only player to appear in more than 500 games at 5 different positions.

Pete was the Reds' field manager from 1984 to '89, compiling a .526 winning percentage. Following the '89 season he was banned from baseball for gambling and was barred from his rightful place in Cooperstown's National Baseball Hall of Fame.

Pete now hosts a syndicated radio talk show from the Pete Rose Ballpark Cafe in beautiful Boca Raton, Florida.

Executive Chef Harold Hayes, of the Pete Rose Ballpark Cafe, was kind enough to share this delicious recipe.

Pete's Artichoke Dip

3 pounds cream cheese
2 (14-ounce) cans artichoke hearts
1/2 cup country-style (whole-grain) Dijon mustard
1/4 cup mayonnaise
2 tablespoons Lowry's or Aunt Jane's seasoning salt
Tortilla chips

Process all ingredients in a food processor, blender, or mixer until well blended. Heat in a microwave until warm, being careful not to overheat.

Serve dip on a large platter with tortilla chips.

The Wit and Wisdom of Dizzy Dean

"For the first twenty years of my life, I never had enough good things to eat and I ain't caught up yet."—Dizzy, when asked about his tremendous appetite for food

"Look at that ol' apple go!"—Dizzy's home-run call as an announcer

"I plan to go down to old Mexico and slay deer, but first I'm goin' to Oklahoma to spend ten days with my mother and eat some of her cornbread."—Dizzy, on his off-season plans following a Cardinals' World Series triumph

"We got some wheat and oats and corn, and I'm gonna have me some cows and chickens and some of them dirty hogs. I liked livin' in Florida, but I couldn't grow me no veg-tuh-bles down there. So pretty soon I'll be eatin' my own tomatoes and green onions."—Dizzy, on his 1939 move to a 154-acre Texas farm

"Give 'em a high fastball and cross 'em up with a hook on the outside, and they're apple pie."—Dizzy's philosophy on pitch selection

Tim Salmon

Photograph courtesy of Tim Salmon and Anaheim Sports

Born and raised in California, Tim Salmon is one of baseball's most talented young players. He was voted Minor League Player of the Year in 1992 and followed that up with a Rookie of the Year season for the California Angels in 1993. And thanks to ESPN's Chris Berman, Tim has one of the big league's most humorous nicknames—"Sockeye."

Salmon is one of the game's most consistent performers and should be a standout for many years to come.

Tim and his wife, Marci, really enjoy the rich casserole creations they sent us for this book.

Two-Step Chicken-Broccoli Casserole

1 pound broccoli, chopped, cooked, and drained
1½ cups cubed cooked chicken
1 can cream of broccoli soup
⅓ cup milk
½ cup shredded cheddar cheese
1 tablespoon melted butter
2 tablespoons dry breadcrumbs

Preheat oven to 450°.

Arrange broccoli in a 9-inch casserole dish and top with chicken.

Combine soup and milk; pour over chicken. Sprinkle with cheese.

Combine butter and breadcrumbs and sprinkle over cheese.

Bake 15 minutes or until hot.

Makes 4 servings.

Enchilada Casserole

1 pound ground beef
Salt
Pepper
Garlic salt
10 corn tortillas
1 small can sliced black olives
1 small can chopped green chiles
1 (10-ounce) can tomato sauce
1 (10-ounce) can enchilada sauce
Grated cheddar cheese

Preheat oven to 350°.

Brown meat and season with salt, pepper, and garlic salt; drain.

Tear corn tortillas and place in bottom of 13 x 9-inch baking dish.

Spread half of meat on top of tortillas. Layer half of the olives and chiles on top of the meat; top with rest of meat, olives, and chiles.

Combine tomato and enchilada sauces and drizzle over layers in dish. Sprinkle grated cheese over top.

Bake 15–20 minutes or until cheese melts.

The Cracker Jack Story

Photograph courtesy of Burson-Marsteller

" **E**at Cracker Jack and Grow Big" proclaimed one early advertisement, and the popularity of this product has grown very big indeed. If the boxes of Cracker Jack sold during its first 100-year-history were lined up end to end, they'd circle the earth more than 63 times!

It all started when F. W. Rueckheim, a German immigrant, came to Chicago with $200 in 1871 and set up a simple popcorn stand. His brother, Louis, left Germany and joined F. W.'s fledgling operation two years later. Sales grew steadily over the next two decades, forcing the brothers to constantly expand their manufacturing space for their increasingly popular "Popcorn Specialties."

The company's biggest break came in 1893 when more than 21 million people from around the world gathered in Chicago for the World's Fair and tasted the brothers' brand-new confection made of peanuts, popcorn, and molasses—the forerunner of Cracker Jack. The product garnered immediate international acclaim.

This newfound success wasn't without its drawbacks however. When the Rueckheims began shipping the product in large, wooden tubs, the candy-coated popcorn stuck together in large clumps. Louis eventually perfected a process to keep each molasses-drenched morsel separate. The process, still in use today, remains a closely-guarded secret.

About 1896 a salesman tasted the sweet snack and declared, "Now that's a Cracker Jack!" This 1890's equivalent of "Totally Awesome" stuck like molasses, in a manner of speaking.

Cracker Jack and baseball became forever entwined in 1908 when composer Albert Von Tilzer and lyricist Jack Norworth penned "Take Me Out to the Ballgame." Every summer fans hear "Buy me some peanuts and Cracker Jacks" at ballparks across the country.

In 1912 F. W. acted on a hunch and started packing a prize in every Cracker Jack box. Prizes in the early years included miniature baseball scoreboards and baseball figures as well as baseball cards. A complete set of original 1915 cards in mint condition has been valued at $60,000. The "Shoeless Joe" Jackson card alone can fetch as much as $7,000! At last count more than 17 billion prizes have been given away, making Cracker Jack the world's largest user of toys.

During World War I Cracker Jack unveiled Sailor Jack and his faithful dog, Bingo. Sailor Jack was modeled after F. W.'s young grandson, who died of pneumonia shortly after the character first appeared on the unique, wax-sealed packages. Sailor Jack and Bingo continue to adorn Cracker Jack boxes as the timeless treat enjoys its second century of popularity.

Jose Santiago

Photograph courtesy of Jose Santiago and the Boston Red Sox

Known as "Palillo" ("Toothpick") to his friends, Jose Santiago was born in Puerto Rico in 1940. His professional baseball career included 3 years in the Major Leagues with the Kansas City Athletics and the Boston Red Sox.

Jose's best seasons came in 1966 and 1967 when he posted 12 wins each campaign. In 1967 Santiago became the first Latin pitcher to start Game 1 of the World Series. He battled the legendary Bob Gibson in a classic pitcher's duel, losing a close 2-1 decision. Boston's only run came when Jose blasted a solo home run off his Hall of Fame opponent.

Jose still plays an active role in baseball. He directs a Puerto Rican baseball academy and serves as a pitching coach in the Chicago Cubs Minor League system.

Jose enjoys golfing and spending time with his wife, Edna, and sons Alex, Albert, Arnold, and Anthony.

A special gracias to Edna Santiago for supplying us with this family recipe.

Chicken Fricassee with Rice

1 whole (3-pound) chicken
1/2 cup pimento-stuffed green olives
5 medium potatoes, peeled and halved
1 small can red peppers
1 medium onion, chopped
1 tablespoon minced garlic
5 bay leaves
1 (8-ounce) can tomato sauce
1/4 cup white or red cooking wine
1 cube chicken bouillon
1 tablespoon cooking oil
1 teaspoon salt
4 1/2 cups water
3 cups uncooked white rice

Cut chicken into pieces and place in a large skillet. Add olives, potatoes, red peppers, onion, garlic, bay leaves, tomato sauce, wine, and bouillon cube. Cook over high heat 5 minutes. Cover skillet, reduce heat, and simmer about 30 minutes or until tender.

Combine cooking oil and salt in medium saucepan. Add water and rice; mix well. Cook over high heat until rice comes to a boil, stirring occasionally. Cover, reduce heat to medium, and cook until top of rice begins to dry out.

Turn rice over gently, but don't stir too much. Cover and cook an additional 10 minutes or until done.

Serve chicken fricassee over rice.

Makes 6 servings.

George Scott

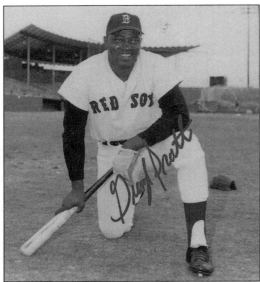

Photograph courtesy of George Scott and the Boston Red Sox

George "Boomer" Scott, a native of Greenville, Mississippi, logged 14 years in the big leagues and blasted 271 lifetime home runs. Boomer spent most of his career in Boston, where he played for the Red Sox in the 1967 World Series. He is said to be the originator of the slang expression "tater," now widely used throughout baseball to describe a home run.

And, folks, Boomer knows taters almost as well as Idaho! In 1975 he led the American League with 36 home runs and 109 runs batted in as a member of the Milwaukee Brewers. He was also considered a very flashy defensive first baseman.

Boomer now lives in New England and manages the Massachusetts Mad Dogs of the independent North Atlantic Baseball League. He always looks forward to returning to the Mississippi Delta and the home-cooked meals of his beloved mother, Magnolia.

Delta Cornbread

¹/₄ cup bacon grease, divided
1 cup flour
4 teaspoons baking powder
¹/₂ teaspoon salt
2 tablespoons sugar
1 cup yellow cornmeal
1 large egg
1 cup milk

Preheat oven to 425°.

Spoon 2 tablespoons bacon grease into cast-iron skillet; place in oven until grease melts and sizzles. Remove skillet from oven and immediately tip to coat inside of skillet evenly with grease.

Stir together flour, baking powder, salt, and sugar until well mixed. Stir in cornmeal.

Beat egg lightly in a separate bowl. Make a well in the middle of the dry ingredients; pour in milk, egg, and remaining bacon grease. Beat mixture for about 1 minute.

Pour batter into the warm, grease-coated skillet and bake 20–25 minutes.

Boomer's Mashed Taters

4 pounds potatoes
1¹/₂ sticks butter or margarine
2 cups half-and-half
1 teaspoon salt
1 teaspoon pepper
Brown gravy

Peel, quarter, and boil potatoes until tender. Drain and mash together with remaining ingredients. Beat until smooth.

Serve with brown gravy.

Andy Seminick

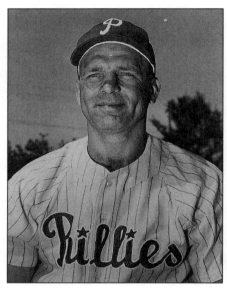

Photograph courtesy of Andy Seminick and the Philadelphia Phillies

W est Virginia native Andy Seminick is best remembered as the catcher for the Phillies' 1950 "Whiz Kids" team. He joined forces with Richie Ashburn, Robin Roberts, and others to lead the Phils to the National League pennant and a World Series showdown with the Yankees.

Andy blasted 164 lifetime homers, including 24 in 1949 and again in 1950. He hit 3 home runs in one 1949 game and was named to the National League All-Star team that season.

Andy now makes his home in Melbourne, Florida.

Venison Stroganoff

1 pound venison, sliced thin and cubed into 3/4-inch pieces
1/4 cup flour
1/2 teaspoon salt
1/2 teaspoon pepper
4 tablespoons cooking oil
1/2 cup chopped onion
1 clove garlic, peeled and minced
1 (6-ounce) can sliced mushrooms, drained
3/4 cup sour cream
1 can cream of tomato soup
1 tablespoon Worcestershire sauce
Cooked rice, noodles, or spaghetti

Dredge venison in flour seasoned with salt and pepper, and brown in hot oil in Dutch oven or deep skillet. Add onion, garlic, and mushrooms.

Combine sour cream, tomato soup, and Worcestershire sauce; pour over meat mixture. Cover and heat to steaming; reduce heat and simmer for about 45 minutes or until meat is tender.

Serve over rice, noodles, or spaghetti.

Enos Slaughter

Photograph courtesy of Enos Slaughter and the St. Louis Cardinals

Born in Roxboro, North Carolina, in 1916, Enos Slaughter was known to his fans and teammates as "Country" because of his rural roots. He spent 19 years in the Major Leagues—15 with the St. Louis Cardinals.

Enos rapped out over 2,300 career hits despite losing three prime years to World War II (1943–45). He was the National League hit leader in 1942 and runs-batted-in king in 1946. Slaughter leads all Hall of Famers with 77 career pinch hits.

Enos played in five World Series, batting .291 with 3 home runs. Cardinal fans still talk about his heads-up base running in Game 7 of the 1946 Fall Classic. Enos raced home from first base on a single with the deciding run as St. Louis dropped the Boston Red Sox.

Enos still lives in his hometown of Roxboro.

Country's Zucchini Bread

3 cups flour
1 teaspoon salt
1 teaspoon baking soda
1/4 teaspoon baking powder
2 teaspoons cinnamon
2 cups sugar
1 cup cooking oil
3 eggs
2 cups grated zucchini
3 teaspoons vanilla
1 cup walnuts, chopped
1/2 cup raisins or 1 (8-ounce) can crushed pineapple
1/2 cup sour cream

Preheat oven to 325°.

In a large bowl mix together flour, salt, baking soda, baking powder, cinnamon, and sugar. Add remaining ingredients and stir well.

Pour batter into 2 well-greased loaf pans.

Bake 1 hour and 10 minutes or until firm.

Makes 2 loaves.

Bobby Thigpen

Photograph courtesy of Bobby Thigpen and the Chicago White Sox

A native of Florida, Bobby Thigpen was a teammate of Will Clark and Rafael Palmeiro during his college days at Mississippi State. A hard-throwing closer, Bobby established the all-time single-season save mark of 57 in 1990 while pitching for the Chicago White Sox.

Bobby appeared in a league high 77 games in 1990, posting a brilliant 1.83 earned run average. All told, Bobby racked up more than 200 career saves.

Away from the ballpark Bobby enjoys deer hunting, fishing, and golf.

Shrimp Spread

2 pounds fresh shrimp
Juice of 1 lemon
1 onion, grated
1 teaspoon curry powder
1/2 cup chopped celery
3/4 cup mayonnaise
Dash of Worcestershire sauce
Salt
Pepper

Boil shrimp; let cool and peel. Grind peeled shrimp in food processor using fine blade.

Combine ground shrimp with remaining ingredients, adding salt and pepper to taste. Mix well.

Place shrimp mixture in small mold or bowl and serve with crackers.

French Silk Chocolate Pie

1 (8-ounce) stick butter
3/4 cup sugar
2 squares unsweetened chocolate, melted
1 teaspoon vanilla
2 eggs
1 baked pie shell
Heavy cream, whipped
Slivered almonds

Cream butter and sugar until fluffy. Blend in chocolate and vanilla; add eggs one at a time, beating for 2 minutes after each addition.

Pour mixture into pie shell and chill for at least 3 hours. Top with whipped cream and almonds.

Charley Timmons–
Ballpark Organist

A native of Chattanooga, Tennessee, Charley Timmons spent 20 seasons as stadium organist for the AA Chattanooga Lookouts of the Southern League. Charley was seldom seen but always heard at historic Engel Stadium, and he holds the dubious distinction of being the first organist to be thrown out of a professional game by an umpire!

This unusual occurrence took place during the 1976 season—Charley's first with the Lookouts. After a couple of questionable calls by Umpire Joe West, Charley played the tune "Three Blind Mice," to the delight of the Chattanooga faithful. Joe wasn't amused and ordered Charley to leave the ballpark. This incident caused such an uproar that Joe required a police escort in order to leave the field safely when the game was over!

Charley's high-tech keyboard cost over $40,000 and is protected by two different alarm systems. Charley has had offers from three different Major League teams, but he is content with Chattanooga and his day job with the city fire department.

Charley says this basic soup is easy to make, inexpensive, and freezes very well.

Charley's Bachelor Soup

1 pound ground beef
2 cups diced carrots
1/2 cup diced celery
1 medium onion, peeled and chopped
1/4 cup uncooked rice
2 teaspoons salt
1/4 teaspoon pepper
1 can crushed tomatoes
4 cups boiling water

Place all ingredients in a large kettle. Cover tightly and bring to a boil; reduce heat and simmer about 1 hour.

Makes 2 quarts.

Hal Trosky

Photograph courtesy of Hal Trosky

Hal was born Harold Troyavesky in Norway, Iowa. During the 1930s he was one of the American League's best hitters and run-producers.

In 1934 Hal broke in with the Cleveland Indians, hitting .330 with 35 homers and 142 runs batted in during his rookie season. His best season came two years later in 1936—all Hal did that year was hit .343 with 216 hits, 42 round-trippers, and 162 runs batted in!

Hal twice clubbed 3 home runs in a game, and he drove in over 100 runs in six consecutive seasons (1934–39). He wrapped up his career as a member of the Chicago White Sox.

Hal passed away in 1979, but his son, Hal Jr., continued the baseball tradition, playing seven years for the White Sox organization.

Hal Trosky Jr., who lives in Cedar Rapids, Iowa, calls himself a "cookin' fanatic." He provided us with these Trosky family recipes.

Bacon and Egg Lasagne

1 pound bacon, cut into 1-inch strips
1 cup chopped onion
1/3 cup flour
1/2 teaspoon salt
1/2 teaspoon pepper
4 cups whole milk
12 lasagne noodles, cooked and drained
12 hard-boiled eggs, sliced
2 cups (8 ounces) shredded Swiss cheese
1/3 cup grated Parmesan cheese
2 tablespoons chopped fresh parsley

Fry bacon in a large skillet until crisp; drain, reserving 1/3 cup drippings. Set fried bacon aside.

Brown onion in bacon drippings until tender. Stir in flour, salt, and pepper to form a paste. Add milk slowly, stirring over medium-low heat until mixture comes to a boil and thickens into a white sauce.

Preheat oven to 350°.

Spoon a small amount of sauce into bottom of a greased 9 x 13-inch baking dish. Divide noodles, bacon, sauce, eggs, and Swiss cheese into thirds, and layer in baking dish, repeating twice. Sprinkle with Parmesan cheese.

Bake 25–30 minutes or until thoroughly heated.

Sprinkle with parsley and let stand 10 minutes before serving.

Pheasant and Wild Rice Casserole

2 pheasants
1 cup wild rice
6 tablespoons butter, divided
1/2 cup chopped onion
1 pound fresh mushrooms, sliced
2 teaspoons salt
1/4 teaspoon freshly ground black pepper
1/2 cup sliced almonds
3 cups chicken broth
1 1/2 cups heavy cream
2–4 tablespoons dry sherry

Cover birds with water in a large stock pan. Boil, covered, about 1 hour or until meat is tender. Let cool; remove meat from bones and cut into bite-size pieces.

Place wild rice in a saucepan, cover with water, and bring to a boil. Remove from heat and allow to soak about 1 hour; drain.

Preheat oven to 350°.

Melt 3 tablespoons butter in a saucepan over medium heat. Saute onion and mushrooms until lightly browned.

In a large bowl, combine pheasant, rice, onion, mushrooms, salt, pepper, almonds, broth, heavy cream, and sherry; mix well. Place mixture into a lightly oiled 2 1/2-quart casserole dish.

Cover and bake 75 minutes.

Cut remaining 3 tablespoons butter into small pieces. Remove cover from casserole dish and spread butter chunks evenly over the top.

Bake uncovered an additional 20 minutes.

As Harry Caray Would Say, "Holy Cow!"

The Big Texan Steak Ranch restaurant in Amarillo, Texas, is famous for its free steak dinners. Anyone who devours the 72-ounce steak as well as a shrimp cocktail, salad, baked potato, and roll—*all within one hour!*—gets the meal free. The customer cannot leave the table unescorted, and a waitress watches closely to make sure every bite is eaten within the required time. Diners who fail must pay the full price, which is about $30.

An unidentified big league player owns the Blazing Fork Award, having polished off the entire feast in just eleven minutes! Sparks flying from his utensils most likely started brushfires throughout the Texas Panhandle.

Bobby Valentine

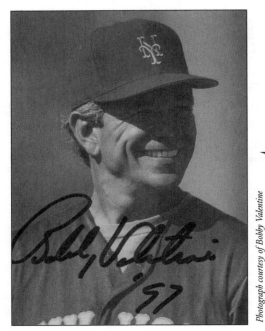

Photograph courtesy of Bobby Valentine

A native of Stamford, Connecticut, Bobby Valentine was a 3-time all-state football standout in high school. He also starred on the baseball diamond and was drafted in the first round by the Los Angeles Dodgers.

During his solid big league playing career, the versatile Valentine wore the uniforms of the Angels, Padres, Mets, and Mariners. Following his retirement as a player, Bobby served briefly as a Mets coach before being appointed manager of the Texas Rangers in 1985. Just 1 year later he had transformed the Rangers into serious contenders and was recognized as the 1986 Major League Manager of the Year.

Bobby went on to coach briefly with the Cincinnati Reds before heading back to the Mets for a lengthy stint in their farm system. In 1995 he packed his bags for Japan, where he piloted the Chiba Lotte Marines to their best finish in team history. On the strength of this outstanding track record, Bobby was named the 16th manager of the New York Mets franchise in August 1996, a position he still holds entering the 1998 season.

Bobby has been an off-season resident of the Arlington, Texas, area since 1986. He operates 4 restaurants under the name *Bobby Valentine's Sports Gallery Cafe* (1 in Texas and 3 in Connecticut). The fare at these popular eateries includes hamburger creations named after Bobby's former and current professional baseball teams.

Bobby V's Bacon, Avocado, and Tomato Pasta

8 strips lean bacon, diced and cooked
1/2 cup finely chopped fresh basil
1/4 cup finely chopped fresh parsley*
1 tablespoon minced fresh garlic
1 teaspoon salt
1 teaspoon white pepper
1/2 teaspoon cayenne pepper (optional)
1/2 teaspoon granulated onion
1/4 cup fresh grated Parmesan cheese*
1/2 cup diced Roma tomatoes
24 ounces spiral pasta, cooked according to package
    directions
1 avocado, peeled, pitted, and diced

Note: Reserve a small amount of the parsley and Parmesan cheese for garnish.

Heat diced cooked bacon over medium heat in a large skillet for 1 minute to release the flavor. Add remaining ingredients except pasta and avocado, reserving some parsley and Parmesan cheese for garnish; stir well.

Add pasta and warm thoroughly; remove from heat. Just before serving, fold diced avocado gently into pasta mixture. Garnish with remaining parsley and Parmesan.

Makes 4 servings.

Bill Virdon

Photograph courtesy of Bill Virdon and the Pittsburgh Pirates

Bill Virdon is a well-respected baseball man who has had a successful career as both a player and manager. Bill wore signature horn-rimmed glasses and served as a dependable outfielder for St. Louis and Pittsburgh from 1955 until 1968.

Bill rapped out 1,596 Major League hits over 12 seasons. He was a member of the 1960 World Champion Pittsburgh Pirates, collecting 7 hits and 5 runs batted in during the 1960 World Series versus the Yankees.

Some fans might recognize Bill as the former manager of the Pirates, Yankees, and Astros. He won 96 games and a divisional title in his first year as a big league skipper with the Bucs in 1972. Bill continues to make an impact as a big league bench coach.

Bill and his wife, Shirley, make their off-season home in Springfield, Missouri.

Shirley Virdon says this recipe has been a favorite of Bill's for years.

Fruit Cocktail Pudding

1 cup sugar
1 cup flour
Pinch of salt
1 teaspoon baking soda
1 medium can fruit cocktail
1 egg
2 teaspoons juice from fruit cocktail
1 teaspoon vanilla
1/4 cup brown sugar
1/2 cup chopped pecans
Whipped cream or vanilla ice cream

Preheat oven to 350°.

Combine sugar, flour, salt, and baking soda in a medium bowl; set aside.

Drain fruit cocktail, reserving juice.

Beat egg well; add drained fruit plus 2 teaspoons of reserved juice. Combine with dry ingredients.

Add vanilla, mixing well. Pour into greased 2-quart casserole dish; spread with brown sugar and sprinkle with chopped pecans.

Bake 30 minutes.

Serve with whipped cream or vanilla ice cream.

Harry Walker

Photograph courtesy of Harry Walker and the Pittsburgh Pirates

Harry "The Hat" Walker was born in Pascagoula, Mississippi, in 1918. You might say he had baseball in his blood—his father was a big league pitcher and his brother, Dixie, enjoyed an 18-year Major League career. In fact the Walker boys were the very first brothers to each win a big league batting crown (Dixie in 1944 and Harry in 1947).

Harry became known as "The Hat" because he adjusted his cap at the plate after each pitch. He is said to have worn out some 20 hats each season!

Harry posted a .296 lifetime average over 15 years and batted a sparkling .412 in the 1946 World Series for the St. Louis Cardinals. He went on to manage 3 different National League clubs (St. Louis, Pittsburgh, and Houston) over 9 seasons.

Harry now resides in Leeds, Alabama.

Bread Pudding with Vanilla Sauce

1 (8-ounce) loaf French bread
1 1/4 cups sugar
1/2 cup brown sugar
1 1/2 teaspoons cinnamon
6 eggs, beaten
1 tablespoon vanilla
1 tablespoon bourbon
Pinch of salt
Pinch of nutmeg
2 cups milk
1 stick butter
2 cups half-and-half
1/2 cup raisins
1/2 apple, peeled and diced into 1/2-inch pieces
Additional raisins
Vanilla Sauce (see recipe below)
Vanilla ice cream

Preheat oven to 325°.

Cut French bread into 1/2-inch cubes; toast in oven until light brown. Remove and set aside.

Increase oven temperature to 350°.

Combine sugars and divide in half. Add cinnamon, eggs, vanilla, bourbon, salt, and nutmeg to half of sugar mixture; stir well and set aside.

Combine remaining half of sugar mixture with milk, butter, and half-and-half. Bring to a boil; whisk into the sugar-egg mixture.

Add raisins, diced apple, and bread cubes; let stand to soak thoroughly. Pour into greased baking dish.

Place dish in pan of hot water and bake 1 hour or until knife inserted in center comes out clean. Sprinkle with raisins and serve warm with Vanilla Sauce and ice cream.

Vanilla Sauce

¹/₆ cup flour
¹/₄ cup sugar
¹/₄ stick butter, cut into small pieces
³/₄ cup boiling water
¹/₂ teaspoon vanilla

Mix flour and sugar in saucepan; add butter.

Add boiling water and cook, stirring constantly, over medium heat until thick. Stir in vanilla.

Makes 6–8 servings.

Harry tells us he uses a large Canada goose for the following recipe, but ducks can be prepared in the same manner.

Harry's Wild Goose Pate

1 large wild goose
Celery seed
1 apple
2 stalks celery
1 small unpeeled onion
2 teaspoons Worcestershire sauce
1 quart mayonnaise
Salt
Melba toast

Preheat oven to 350°.

Rub goose inside and out with celery seed; place apple inside.

Bake about 1¹/₂–2 hours or until goose is tender. Let cool; remove meat from bones and grind in meat grinder or food processor.

Grind celery and onion, and mix with ground goose.

Add Worcestershire sauce, mayonnaise, and salt to taste.

Serve with melba toast.

Recipe Index

Appetizers

Breads

Desserts

Main Dishes

Salads

Side Dishes

Miscellaneous